Yesterday's HIGHWAYS

The Great American Road Trip

Stephen H. Provost

All material © 2020 Stephen H. Provost
Cover concept and design: Stephen H. Provost
Interior design: Stephen H. Provost
All contemporary photographs © 2020 Stephen H. Provost, except where noted.
Historical images are in the public domain, except where noted.

No part of this book may be reproduced, or stored in a retrieval system, or transmitted in any form or by any means, electronic, mechanical, photocopying, recording, or otherwise, without the express written permission of the publisher.

Dragon Crown Books 2020

All rights reserved.

ISBN: 978-1-949971-10-1

Dedication

To my fellow travelers along America's highways and byways:
If you've ever searched out sections of abandoned pavement,
spent the night at a roadside motel with a neon sign flashing
outside your window, counted gas stations or billboards,
grabbed some chicken nuggets at a truck stop,
or stopped at an all-night diner for a cuppa joe, this one's for you.

Contents

Introduction   7
Highway Fever   9
All Pumped Up   45
Keep on Truckin'   89
Eat at Joe's   99
Room at the Inn   143
Ride on the Weird Side   169
Have Fun, Will Travel   189
Big Ads   211
Falling Down   235
Hey! This Way!   247

More Reading

Check out these other great highway-themed books by the author.

Roy's Café, motel and gas station is still open in Amboy, Calif., along U.S. 66. Amboy is a ghost town today: It shriveled up after Interstate 40 bypassed Route 66. But Roy's survives as a destination/tourist attraction for those interested in revisiting the history of the Mother Road.

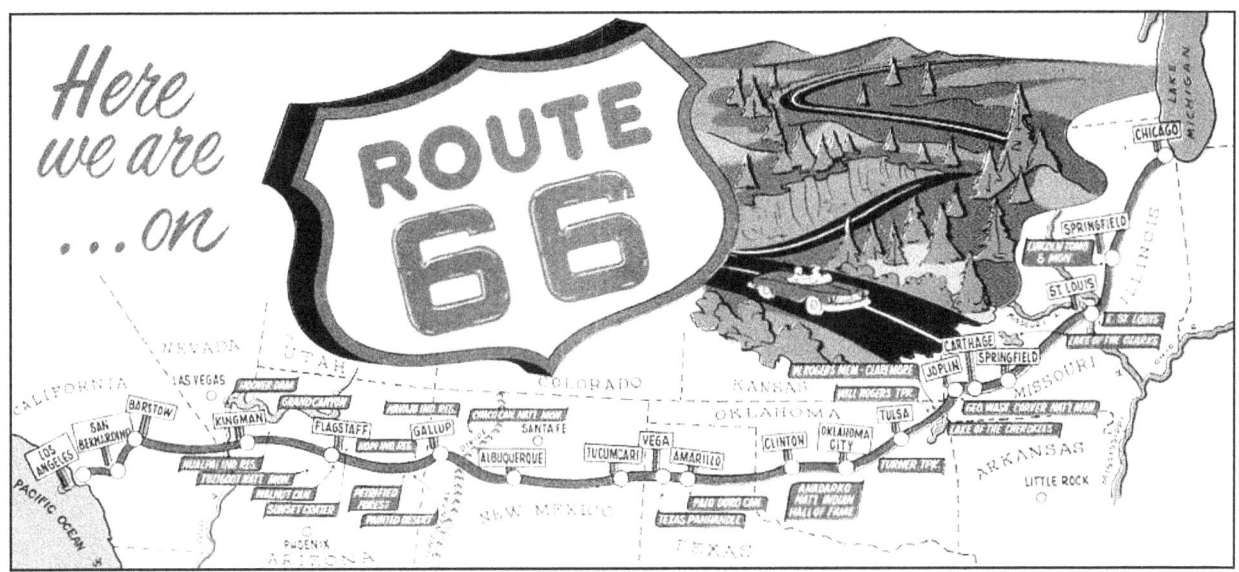

Introduction

When Tom Cochrane released a song called *Life is a Highway* in 1991, it struck a chord with American listeners, reaching the top ten on the Billboard Hot 100. It's no wonder, because highways have long been a big part of American life. The typical driver spends about an hour behind the wheel each day, which works out to more than *two years* during an average lifespan (more if you face a daily commute in a big city).

Nostalgia drives many highway enthusiasts toward Route 66, the "Mother Road," which served as a conduit for adventurers, migrants and vacationers during the mid-20th century. This road from Chicago to Los Angeles was so famous it spawned a TV show that ran for four seasons on CBS in the early 1960s. By that time, however, the famed cross-country thoroughfare was already doomed to obsolescence by President Dwight Eisenhower's interstate highway system.

The golden age of the open road is indelibly etched in the memories of baby boomers. As hard as it may be to believe, it lasted only three short decades, from 1926 to 1956. But it was an era of rapid and defining change in the nation's history. The Mother Road and the rest of the U.S. highway system were dedicated amid the optimism of the Roaring Twenties, then bore witness to the Dust Bowl, the Great Depression, World War II, the postwar return to prosperity and the Cold War. By the time the interstate system had fully replaced it, the Vietnam era was in full swing. Perhaps at no time during our nation's history had so much of consequence happened so fast, and we witnessed it all from the driver's seat on the open road.

Some of it remains visible today, and if you don't have the luxury of getting behind the wheel to tour the fast-disappearing highways of yesteryear, you can still see some of the sights in the pages that follow. This is not intended to be a comprehensive survey of the American road, but a series of highlights — a taste of what it was like to drive along Route 66 or the Lincoln Highway, the Lee Highway or El Camino Real.

Whether you were traveling in a 1932 Ford Roadster, a '51 Hudson Hornet or a '63 Buick Riviera (the best-selling car the year I was born), you'd need the same things: a cup of coffee, a hearty meal, gas in your tank and a place to spend the night. And there were hundreds of businesses on the roadside ready to cater to those needs.

Many of them are gone today, bypassed by modern interstates that have transformed more than a few highway stops into mini-ghost towns. Some continue to hang on, bringing in just enough business to survive, or finding new life as purveyors of nostalgia that specialize in coffee mugs and T-shirts. The remnants of others linger, abandoned, in a roadside graveyard of cracked asphalt parking lots, hollowed-out buildings and signs that point to nowhere.

I went searching for these vestiges of the American highway's golden age. The pages that follow contain just some of what I found.

Roads and Bridges

Route 66 through the Mojave Desert in California.

Highway Fever

Like the nation itself, America's highways are always evolving. They started as dirt trails, blazed by Native Americans and followed by European settlers on horseback and in wagons.

By the 1800s, a few had become gravel roads, heavily traveled by merchants moving goods between coastal ports and the inland frontier. In the early 20th century, with the advent of the motorcar, they became auto trails and then, in 1926, links in the first federal highway system.

These early highways were surface streets through town, the old "Main Street" or "Front Street," cobbled together and linked by narrow country roads made of everything from clay to gravel to concrete in a few brief stretches.

Over time, they grew wider (and busier), eventually giving way to modern interstate highways. Today, ribbons of asphalt bypass the cities and towns that gave them birth, rushing ahead on the tide of history.

Amazingly, though, many still follow those paths first trod by Native Americans centuries ago — paths through lush and scenic valleys, across high mountain passes and backward into the mists of time.

The Great Wagon Road

One such highway was the Great Wagon Road down the East Coast, which — as its name, the Great Warriors' Road, suggests — predated the automobile and, like many others, followed a Native American trail in use long before the arrival of European settlers.

The road began in Philadelphia and made its way east to Gettysburg, where it turned south across a narrow strip of Maryland and into Virginia. At Big Lick (modern Roanoke), it split in two, with the main road continuing south toward Charlotte in North Carolina and ultimately to Augusta in Georgia. The other branch, called the Wilderness Road, turned westward and split in two again: One road swung northwest through the Cumberland Gap into Kentucky and toward the Ohio River; the other continued west to Knoxville, Tenn.

Anyone who's traveled modern highways through the region has traced these routes, perhaps without even knowing it.

A stretch of U.S. Highway 30 from Philadelphia to Gettysburg follows a segment of the old Lincoln Highway, which in turn paralleled this section of the Great Wagon Road. For the next major stretch, down to Roanoke, U.S. 11 and the more modern Interstate 81 both run along alongside the old native trail, then follow the Wilderness Trail into Tennessee. South of Roanoke, portions of U.S. 220, Interstate 285, I-85 and I-77 roughly follow the path of the Great Wagon Road.

In northwest Virginia, it was known as the Great Valley Road: the "valley" in question being the Shenandoah Valley, where it served as a vital commercial corridor. In fact, it was so well-traveled that it was only a matter of time before the road itself became a source of profit. If the road could be improved, more merchants could use it — and they could get from one place to another more quickly.

YESTERDAY'S HIGHWAYS

To this end, the Valley Turnpike Company was formed in the 1830s to upgrade sixty-eight miles of the trail by straightening it, building bridges, and laying down a macadamized surface over the rutted mud and dirt. Macadam was a relatively new development at the time. It was a level surface of crushed and compacted stone developed by Scottish engineer John McAdam around 1820. (Today, most travelers would probably refer to macadamized routes simply as "gravel roads.")

In the United States, McAdam's technique had first been used in 1823 on the a ten-mile stretch of road in Maryland. It was employed again a couple of years later on a more ambitious project: 73 miles of what would later be called the National Road. That project took five years to complete, with the road itself eventually stretching from Cumberland, Md., to Vandalia, Ill. It was the first major improved highway to be funded by the federal government — although Congress later turned it over to the states because it was too expensive to maintain. Still, it would endure, eventually serving as the basis for U.S. Highway 40, one of the original federal highways dedicated in 1926.

The Valley Turnpike Company was just one of many private firms getting into the highway business in the first part of the 19th century. By 1830, more than 10,000 miles of turnpikes had been laid down, mostly on the East Coast. Companies paid for the projects by selling stock, then paying their investors through tolls collected along the way from people who used their roads.

The name "turnpike" came from the toll gates installed at regular intervals: These gates were turnstiles consisting of a vertical pole and two crossed bars.

For the Shenandoah Valley project, the Valley Turnpike Company sold $250,000 worth of stock at $25 a share. The cost had increased to $425,000 by 1840 — more than $11 million in 2019 dollars — by which time the company had added another 25 miles of macadamized road to the original length.

It wasn't a cheap road to build, and it wasn't a cheap road to travel, either. Tolls were collected every five miles, and it would have cost nearly $100 in today's dollars to get from one end to the other in 1840. For merchants transporting goods, it was a cost of doing business.

Although the turnpike wasn't a government road, the Commonwealth of Virginia was involved in its upkeep, because it owned 40% of the stock. Unfortunately for all concerned, the Civil War brought north-south commerce to a screeching halt. Making matters worse, the Confederate Army tore up the road and wrecked a number of bridges

— while paying only one-quarter of the usual toll. And when the South lost the war, the Valley Turnpike Company wound up with $20,000 in worthless government bonds on its hands.

By this time, the railroad was fast replacing the turnpike as the preferred mode of commercial transit. Virginia had just 140 miles of railroad in 1840, but four decades later, the figure was closing in on 2,000. Where the Wilderness and Great Valley roads met in Roanoke, the Norfolk & Western and Shenandoah Valley rail lines now converged.

Rail freight cars could carry far bigger loads than horse-drawn wagons, could cover greater distances and could deliver their freight faster. Soon, rail lines were the defining form of transportation linking cities and towns, with the golden spike linking eastbound and westbound rail lines in Utah during the spring of 1869.

It would be roughly a half-century before highways would match the feat of the railroads by creating a truly transcontinental road, but that didn't mean the need for roads had disappeared.

Soon, they would be at the forefront of both commerce and culture once again.

Major Trails Pre-20th Century

Name	Starting point	Destination	Open
King's Highway	Boston	Charleston, S.C.	1650
Boston Post Road	New York	Boston	1673
Fall Line Road	Fredericksburg, Va.	Georgia	1735
Natchez Trace	Natchez, Miss.	Nashville, Tenn.	1742
Great Valley Road	Philadelphia	Augusta, Ga.	1744
El Camino Real	San Diego	San Francisco	1769
Zane's Trace	Wheeling, W.V.	Maysville, Ky.	1805
National Road	Cumberland, Md.	Vandalia, Ill.	1818
Santa Fe Trail	Franklin, Mo.	Santa Fe, N.M.	1821
Oregon Trail	Independence, Mo.	Oregon City, Ore.	1841
California Trail	Independence, Mo.	Sacramento, Calif.	1841
Mormon Trail	Nauvoo, Ill.	Salt Lake City, Utah	1846
Cherokee Trail	Salina, Okla.	Fort Bridger, Wyo.	1849

The Good Roads Movement

Railroads were all well and good for major trips, but you simply couldn't lay down enough rails to get you everywhere you needed to go. It was one thing to travel from, say, Chicago to St. Louis on the B&O Line, but it was quite another to take a trip into town from the farm. For that, you needed a country road.

And in the late 19th century, most Americans still lived on the farm — or at least out in the country. Fully 85% of the population was rural in 1850, and more than half the nation would remain outside the cities until the end of World War I.

The irony was this: Rural residents relied on country roads to take them where the railroads didn't go, but the farther away from the rail lines you got, the worse the roads were.

This posed a problem for the newest craze: the bicycle.

Riders and manufacturers both had an interest in improving the quality of the American road, so they joined in common cause to form the League of American Wheelmen in 1880. This group founded what became known as the Good Roads Movement to enlist the help of farmers, newspapers and politicians in improving the nation's trails, as they were often called.

Farmers were particularly important, because they were most affected by the state of rural roads. Little more than muddy, rutted trails, these unmarked cart paths were often full of holes and washed out by flash floods, leaving farmers with no way to get their goods to market.

An 1891 pamphlet titled *The Gospel of Good Roads* bore the subtitle *A Letter to the American Farmer*. And that's precisely what it was (although it was, at 73 pages, a rather long letter). The tract included photos showing carts stuck halfway up their wagon wheels in mud, along with vivid descriptions of just how bad the situation was. "Here is the picture," the writer stated plainly: "You see the wagon has become hopelessly stuck, and is abandoned by horse and driver. If that horse could talk, what a story we might have!"

One such story involved some farmers from Pennsylvania who needed a six-horse team to transport a single load of hay. The mud was so bad that one of them stumbled and fell in the morass and ended up drowning. The pamphlet went on to describe the cost of enduring bad roads, not just in human life and limb, but also on the business side of things:

"A little while ago, a very clever and intelligent citizen of Indiana estimated that bad roads cost the farmer $15 per year for each horse and mule in his service. This means an aggregate loss of $250 million per year." And that was just the beginning. Once wear and tear on wagons and harnesses was factored in, together with depreciated loss in the value of farmland, the total bill soared to $2.35 billion — at least according to the pamphlet.

The argument was clear: If farmers wanted to save money, they'd have to invest in better roads.

The Age of the Automobile

But the movement didn't really take off until the age of the automobile.

The arrival of this new invention changed everything.

Karl Benz built his first Benz Patent-Motorwagen in 1885, and Gottlieb Daimler sold his first car in 1892: a revamped stagecoach equipped with an engine. By the turn of the century, there were 8,000 privately owned cars, and that number quadrupled in just four years' time.

Soon, everyone wanted in on the action.

But despite the fitful progress made by the Good Roads Movement, there were hardly any decent roads on which to drive. Most people stayed in town, and traveling any distance meant taking the train. Roadmaps were hard to find, and those that did exist were often wrong. The roads themselves weren't marked, unless you counted a splash of paint on a fencepost or a homemade sign on the side of a barn.

So, in 1902, nine local clubs came together in Chicago and formed the American Automobile Association. That same year, Charles and Lucy Glidden became the first motorists to circle the globe in a motorcar. AAA paved the way for better roads in two major ways: by installing roadside markers and by organizing "road runs" — in which Glidden would play a key role.

Just a few months after the group formed, it decided on its first major event: a road tour to the 1904 World's Fair in St. Louis. It wasn't a race. The purpose was to promote the idea of cross-country motoring, so drivers were encouraged to travel at their own pace and enjoy the scenery while testing their vehicles under a variety of road conditions. Three major routes were chosen, beginning in New York, Philadelphia and Baltimore, with other drivers taking secondary routes from Minneapolis, Birmingham and Kansas City.

A total of 77 cars participated (66 of them made it to the end), with the New York contingent being the largest: 18 cars set out from the Big Apple, and five more from Boston joined the group in Albany. Among the latter group was a 24-horsepower Napier driven by Glidden, who had worked with Alexander Graham Bell to pioneer the telephone exchange.

The New York convoy covered 1,350 miles, making it to St. Louis in 18 days. Along the way, the motorists stopped in various towns, meeting with local residents and officials to publicize the tour. Pilot cars traveled ahead of the main group, spreading the word and laying down confetti in the roadway to mark the course.

The enterprise was such a success that a second tour was planned for the following year, but this time, there would be more on the line. Instead of a leisurely drive, the sequel would be an actual race. The idea was to attract sponsorships from fledgling car companies eager to prove that their product was the best and most reliable. The biggest sponsor, though, turned out to be Glidden, who donated a $2,000 trophy for the winner of what would become an annual event.

The Glidden tours, as they were known, continued through 1913, but they weren't without their challenges. Not everyone along the tour routes was eager to welcome the motorists, who were seen by some residents as a nuisance and by local law enforcement as perfect candidates for speed traps. The *New Hampshire Union* lamented that "the lives and property of perfectly harmless people have been seriously menaced; the laws willfully disregarded; and for no earthly reason rather than to afford amusement to a lot of strangers." In one case, the newspaper reported, an old man had injured his arm after being thrown out from his wagon, and his horse had run away. In another, a motorist had been hurt in a collision with a lumber wagon.

Practical jokers would remove the confetti used to mark the proper route or, worse still, scatter it in the wrong direction, leading drivers on a wild goose chase into the hinterlands.

Getting lost wasn't just a problem for motorists on the Glidden tours: It was something that happened to almost everyone who got behind the wheel in those early years. Routes shifted frequently, bad weather turned roads into swamps or dead ends, and directions were poorly marked. Drivers were told to "turn right at the white-painted fencepost" or "keep going past the third barn" — which was hard enough in good weather. But what if a heavy rain washed the paint off that fencepost? What if the wind knocked it over, and what if the farmer tore down that barn?

The answer, clearly, was a more stable and consistent system of road signs and maps, which is what AAA set out to produce. In the absence of any government program to mark the nation's roads, AAA began installing wooden signs (porcelain came later) to mark the way in 1906. It expanded the program a few years later, installing 4,000 signs over one stretch of road between Kansas City and Los Angeles in 1914.

Auto Trails

It was around this time, as the 20th century entered its second decade, that the idea of transcontinental auto trails began to pick up steam. The Good Roads Movement remained active, shifting its focus from cycling to motorcars, but it was no longer a voice crying in the proverbial wilderness. As the automobile became more popular (and, with the arrival of the Model-T in 1908, more affordable), others began to clamor for a stake in the game.

The game, as always, was profit: for car companies, roadside businesses, merchants transporting goods, fuel companies... you name it. Auto trails may have been the forerunners of the first federal highway system, but they were still privately funded — paid for by businessmen who saw them as a way to line their pockets.

And the more different segments of the business world began jockeying for a piece of the action, the more they came into conflict with one another. Disputes were covered in the pages of local newspapers, where disagreements were aired over exactly how the nation's highways would be laid out — and who would do it. Merchants moving goods from one place to another naturally favored the most direct routes. But businesses in cities along the way wanted traffic diverted to pass by their front doorsteps. Travelers, meanwhile, were divided: Some wanted to get where they were going as quickly as possible, while others preferred a scenic jaunt.

Competing trails arose, sponsored by different groups of businesses, and motorists were left to navigate a tangled maze of city streets and rural roads that were cobbled together to form a so-called "highway."

Multiple auto trails started off in New York or the nation's capital, and several wound up on the opposite coast in San Diego or San Francisco. In between however, they were markedly different. On the north-south grid, more than one highway ended up in Miami, a popular destination for winter "snowbirds."

It wasn't as if much new pavement was being laid down; in most cases, businessmen were simply slapping a new name on a meandering sequence of existing roads, which they had chosen to benefit themselves more than the traveler. With the AAA sign-making effort still very much in its infancy, the old "paint on the fencepost" sign system was updated along many of these routes to help motorists stay on the right track. Each auto trail had its own square or rectangular symbol, usually painted on telephone poles along the way:

- The Lincoln Highway featured a blue "L" sandwiched between a red stripe on top and a blue stripe below.
- The Bankhead Highway had the letters "BH" at its center, with a yellow stripe on top and bottom.
- The Lee Highway's logo consisted of the letters "LEE" running diagonally in blue against a white background, with diagonal blue stripes on top and bottom.
- The Dixie Overland Highway's symbol featured the letters "DOH" in blue, superimposed on a white map of the continental United States, against a blue backdrop.
- The Jefferson Highway had blue stripes at top and bottom, with the letters "JH" run together in the center, also in blue, against a white background.
- The Pacific Highway's symbol was simpler: a black stripe between two white stripes at top and bottom; and the Atlantic Highway had the same pattern, except with a red stripe in the middle.

Major Auto Trails

Name	Starting point	Destination
Atlantic Highway	Fort Kent, Maine	Miami
Bankhead Highway	Washington, D.C.	San Diego
Dixie Highway	Sault Ste. Marie, Mich.	Miami
Dixie Overland Highway	Savannah, Ga.	San Diego
Jefferson Highway	Winnipeg, Manitoba (Canada)	New Orleans
Lee Highway	Washington, D.C.	San Diego
Lincoln Highway	New York	San Francisco
National Old Trails Road	Baltimore	San Francisco
Old Spanish Trail	St. Augustine, Fla.	San Diego
Pacific Highway	Vancouver, B.C. (Canada)	San Diego
Victory Highway	New York	San Francisco
Yellowstone Trail	Plymouth, Mass.	Seattle

The Lincoln Highway symbol on a telephone pole in Sutherland, Neb.

The most ambitious of these projects was the Lincoln Highway, in part because it proposed laying down a lot of new pavement (instead of merely cobbling together existing roads) and in part because it was heavily promoted by a man named Carl Fisher.

Fisher had opened the nation's first car dealership in Indianapolis and had helped develop the Indianapolis Motor Speedway, home to the Indy 500. The track debuted in 1909 with a hot-air balloon race, which went off without a hitch. When the cars took to the track, however, it was a different story: It soon became apparent that the gravel-dirt-and-oil surface wouldn't stand up to the pounding of high-speed racing. According to one account, driving on the track was like "flying through a meteor shower" of gravel. Drivers wound up covered with dirt, oil and tar.

One driver was blinded halfway through the opening day's main event when a stone hit his goggles; a second driver was killed, along with his mechanic, when his car flipped and crashed into a fencepost.

The second day of the three-day event went off without incident, but on the third day, one car flew into the crowd and killed three people (two spectators and the mechanic; the lucky driver survived with minor injuries). The race continued, but was called off three-quarters of the way through when another driver hit a pothole and spun into a bridge support.

The driver was uninjured, but the backlash was fierce and immediate: One press report declared that auto racing was more brutal than bullfighting or gladiator games. Fisher responded with a complete overhaul of the facility that included a new concrete wall to protect spectators and a new track made entirely of bricks: 3.2 million of them at 10 pounds each.

That's how the speedway came to be called "The Brickyard."

Interestingly enough, bricks were also used on some sections of Fisher's next project, the Lincoln Highway.

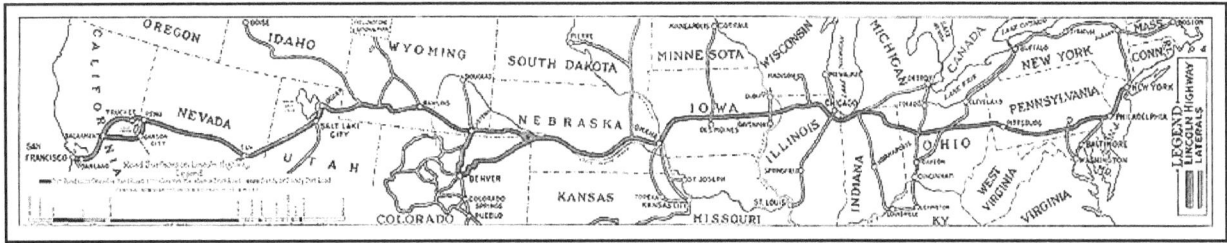

A map shows the route of the Lincoln Highway in 1916.

Surface Tension

It was still very much an open question as to *how* roads should be constructed. Dirt and macadam remained the dominant surfaces as the new century dawned. John McAdam's original "formula" for paving a road had called for three layers of stone laid across a slight slope, with ditches on either side for drainage. Later engineers filled the gaps between the stones with a mixture of dirt and water, but when this dried, it created a lot of dust.

In order to keep the dust down, construction crews began spraying a layer of tar on the road, creating a new kind of surface called "tarmac" ("tar" plus "macadam").

In the Pacific Northwest, a man named Sam Hill used his 7,000-acre ranch near the Columbia River as a testing ground for different road surfaces, shelling out $100,000 to test segments of concrete and asphalt and various kinds of macadam to see which proved the most durable.

A remaining segment of the old wood plank road in the Algodones Dunes, running parallel to modern Interstate 8, east of San Diego.

Concrete was the material of choice for the first Ridge Route across the Tehachapi Mountains, connecting northern and southern California. The two-lane road across the ridgeline supplied the traveler with breathtaking views of the surrounding wilderness, but its myriad twists and turns limited drivers to a maximum speed of 15 miles per hour. It was replaced by a more direct route that was part of U.S. Highway 99 in the early 1930s and, after that, by modern Interstate 5.

Elsewhere, wooden roads were built. A plank road was the solution of choice for a stretch of highway more than six miles long in the desert east of San Diego. It wasn't uncommon for high winds to blow the shifting sands of Algodones Dunes across the path that had been chosen for a new road into Arizona. The solution was a raised road of wooden planks, held together with iron bands. The 8-foot-wide road required turnouts every quarter-mile to allow for passing, but that didn't help drivers it the zero-visibility conditions that arose during sandstorms. Cars often went of the road and had to be abandoned. Ultimately, the plank road was abandoned in 1926 and replaced with a paved, raised road.

Another plank road — consisting of three wooden causeways — was built along the California coast between Ventura and Santa Barbara in 1912. It was meant to allow drivers narrow path between the sheer mountainsides to the east and the Pacific Ocean to the west. The road couldn't stand the pounding of the waves for long and was replaced 12 years after it opened with a paved road that ran over earth fill.

When it came to building the Lincoln Highway, Carl Fisher knew he couldn't pave more than 3,000 miles of his dream project all at once. He didn't have that kind of cash. He helped form the Lincoln Highway Association, which raised $1 million for the construction in 1912 — not nearly enough. Still, the new coast-to-coast highway was dedicated the following year, with most of it being a simple trail of gravel and (in many places) dirt.

In most places, it wasn't much to look at. But Fisher resolved to use the $1 million he had in hand to demonstrate what it could become. He arranged to pave a series of "seedling miles" to showcase the new road's potential, hoping investors would catch the buzz and throw their money behind the venture. The first seedling mile was set down in the unlikely village of Malta, Ill., 70 miles west of Chicago. Just 450 people lived there around the time the concrete dried in 1914.

Grand Island, Neb., got a seedling mile the following year, thanks to a donation of $1,170 from a local man named Fred W. Aston. It's still visible today, having been bypassed by a new highway alignment in 1931, and is the only remaining seedling mile that hasn't been widened or covered with asphalt.

A painted fence along the Lincoln Highway in Sutherland, Neb.

Top: A "seedling mile" of the Lincoln Highway in Grand Island, Neb. **Above:** A section of brick road on the Lincoln Highway west of Omaha. **Left:** A concrete marker.

YESTERDAY'S HIGHWAYS

A few sections of the highway weren't concrete, but brick. Among them: an 18-mile section west of Omaha, part of which is still visible today (see previous page), a fitting memorial to the man behind both the Lincoln Highway and the "Brickyard" at the Indianapolis Motor Speedway.

The Lincoln Highway, like many other auto trails, was incorporated into the first federal highway system, launched in 1926. But in almost every case, the old named trails were partitioned among a variety of state and federal numbered routes. Today, if you want to follow the Lincoln Highway from one coast to the other, you'll have to take parts of seven U.S. highways to get there (although much of the old route follows current U.S. 30).

The Jefferson Highway, meanwhile, has been partitioned among no fewer than 17 highways; the Lee Highway has been split among 10; and the National Old Trails Road shares parts of eight.

Over the years, some routes have been altered, others abandoned and still others bypassed. Remnants, however, are still visible, sometimes through quiet neighborhoods and often alongside modern highways.

Dead Man's Curve, a cut-off section of the Old Ridge Route in California, was a 15-foot-wide slab of concrete replaced by the Ridge Route Alternate (U.S. 99) and, ultimately, Interstate 5.

Clockwise from top left: A section of cracked concrete from the old Cuesta Grade, a part of El Camino Real (U.S. 101) north of San Luis Obispo, Calif.; Sylvan Road in Wooster, Ohio, a residential street that once served as a brick section of the Lincoln Highway; a dead-end concrete section of the old Lincoln Highway just off U.S. 34 in Fort Morgan, Colo.

YESTERDAY'S HIGHWAYS

Bridging the Gap

Bridges were almost as important as good roads — more so in some places — when it came to guaranteeing a safe and smooth trip. In some places, roads were repeatedly washed away by seasonal streams; in others, travelers had to take the long way around (sometimes, a *very* long way) to skirt established waterways. When building the road that would connect the northern and southern halves of California, the state studied three potential routes. The one that ran through a series of valleys and canyons was rejected, in part, because floods repeatedly washed out the dirt trail they hoped to follow. In the end, they decided it was easier to go *over* the mountains, via the ridgeline, even though it involved more than 600 curves and tested early cars' ability to climb the steep hills without overheating.

The long-term solution to rivers and seasonal streams was to build bridges.

Early bridges, like early highways, were private affairs. On the Great Valley Road in Virginia, bridges were part of the improvements funded by the Valley Turnpike Company. In California, lawmakers created a program in 1874 that gave counties the power to set up road districts and pass property taxes for road construction — including bridges. But building bridges wasn't enough: The bridges had to be *safe*. So, in 1893, the state passed a law requiring counties to consult a surveyor before actually building a new bridge.

Many early bridges were built from wood. Among them, especially in the East, were covered bridges. The reason behind them was plain: Winter weather could be harsh, and putting "roofs" on bridges protected the main structure from snow and rain. They kept the timbers underneath from getting soaked and rotting. (They also kept horses from being spooked by river waters rushing by underneath.) A covered bridge could last a century — five times as long as a bridge exposed to the elements.

The first covered bridge in America, the Waterford Bridge, spanned the Hudson River in New York. It was built in 1804 and lasted 105 years. Two more covered spans followed in Oregon City, but both were soon washed away by floodwaters. More covered bridges were built in Pennsylvania and Ohio than anywhere else in the U.S. — 1,500 went up between 1820 and 1900 in Pennsylvania, which also boasted the nation's longest covered bridge at more than a mile, in Lancaster County. Built in 1814, it was destroyed by high water and ice 18 years later. As many as 3,500 covered bridges, meanwhile, were built in Ohio.

Most have disappeared. They've either been washed away, fallen down or been replaced by more modern spans. In Virginia, they were known as "kissing bridges." The 80-foot Bob White Covered Bridge on the Smith River in the rural Virginia town of Woolwine was built in 1921. It was one of only seven public covered bridges remaining in the state when it was washed away by floodwaters in 2015. Just a short distance away, another covered bridge remains: Jack's Creek Bridge (below) just west of State Highway 8. The 48-foot bridge was built in 1914 to serve Jack's Creek Primitive Baptist Church. Known as a queen post truss bridge, it uses two vertical "queen posts" to support a pitched roof.

YESTERDAY'S HIGHWAYS

Most of the nation's wooden covered bridges were built between 1825 and 1875. As cars replaced horse-drawn wagons as the dominant mode of transportation in the early 20th century, sturdier materials were needed. Builders turned to steel and reinforced concrete.

The Bridgehunter website has counted 31,500 truss bridges nationwide, while arch bridges were also plentiful, at more than more than 11,600. There were far fewer suspension bridges, such as the Golden Gate — not even 700 of them. Other types include movable bridges (more than 2,800) and the aforementioned covered bridges (more than 1,500).

The truss design was the overwhelming choice for railroad bridges during the 19th century, but it was used for highways, too. Many have been retired but remain visible alongside newer concrete spans.

The Lake Overholser Bridge, a steel truss span over the North Canadian River, was built as a section of Route 66 in 1924. It was mentioned in John Steinbeck's novel *The Grapes of Wrath*.

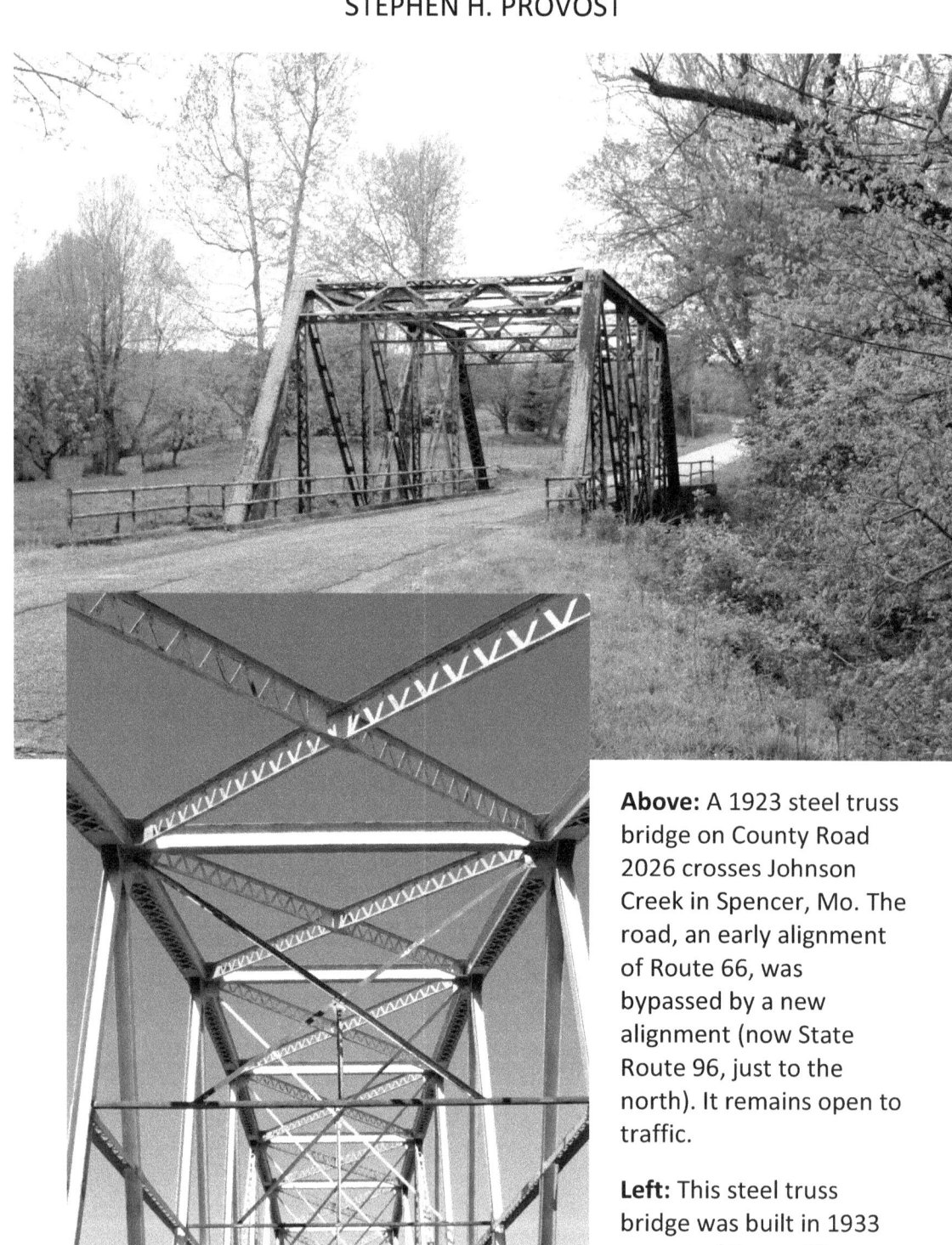

Above: A 1923 steel truss bridge on County Road 2026 crosses Johnson Creek in Spencer, Mo. The road, an early alignment of Route 66, was bypassed by a new alignment (now State Route 96, just to the north). It remains open to traffic.

Left: This steel truss bridge was built in 1933 as part of Route 66 over Rio Puerco. It was remodeled in 1957 and bypassed in 1999.

YESTERDAY'S HIGHWAYS

Left: The Devil's Elbow Truss Bridge over Big Piney River on Teardrop Road (an old alignment of Route 66), was built in 1923 and bypassed in 1942.

Below: The 1924 Walnut Canyon Bridge on an old alignment of Townsend-Winona Road (another old 66 alignment) in Coconino County, Ariz., is no longer open to vehicle traffic. Drivers would cross the bridge en route to Flagstaff.

This 1933 bridge over Little Cabin Creek on old Route 66 in Craig County, Okla., is an example of a pony truss bridge: one not joined by cross braces at the top.

Some bridges weren't bridges at all, but rather, culverts: tunnel-like structures that allow water drainage to pass underneath. These short spans, usually less than 20 feet across, often consist of concrete slabs embedded in the ground, which bear most of the structure's weight. They allow water to flow under the roadway, rather than stretching the road *over* the water.

Culverts aren't as impressive or glamorous as bridges, but they're essential to getting traffic over seasonal waterways that would otherwise wash away roads during winter. Some travel through pipes laid under the roadway.

Even as engineers were building bridges along highways, they were also building culverts.

A concrete culvert on Mountain House Road, an old alignment of U.S. 101 between Cloverdale and Hopland in Northern California carries two dates: 1912, when the original culvert was built, and 1932, when it was improved.

Some of the most challenging seasonal floods occurred near Sacramento, where the ground turned to swampland for miles during the winter. If you were traveling from San Francisco to the state capital, you'd have to head southeast toward Tracy and go all the way to Stockton before heading north again. Distance from Stockton to Sacramento: roughly 50 miles. This was, in fact, the path followed by the initial alignment of the Lincoln Highway.

The Yolo Plankroad, a raised road of wooden planks, built in 1855 to help travelers cross the Davis Wetlands, was an early solution. But it was still vulnerable to flooding: A stage stop/hotel at the west end of the plank road was built on stilts as a precaution, but even this wasn't enough to save it when the waters rose too far, too fast during a flood in 1862.

The plank road was eventually abandoned and replaced by an overland road that could only be used during the summer months. It wasn't until 1916, when the 3.2-mile Yolo Causeway — then the longest concrete bridge in the United States — was built. An immediate push was made to include the new engineering marvel as part of the Lincoln Highway, but the Lincoln Highway Association resisted the idea. (The group finally relented in and changed its route in 1928.)

The causeway was widened to four lanes with the addition of a timber viaduct in 1933.

The Yolo Causeway offered motorists a way across the Davis Wetlands west of Sacramento without having to drive south through Stockton. The causeway was later part of U.S. Highway 99 and has since been incorporated into Interstate 80.

The first modern concrete bridge was built in France in 1840, but it was three decades (1871) before the first such structure went up in the United States, in Prospect Park, Brooklyn.

It wasn't long after the first cars hit the road that grand arching concrete bridges began appearing along U.S. highways, spanning deep gorges, stretching across wide rivers and spanning rail lines. One of the most impressive early concrete arch bridges was the Melan Bridge across the Kansas River in Topeka. When it opened in 1898, it was hailed as the first bridge of its kind built west of the Mississippi and the largest concrete bridge in the United States.

The first bridge at that location had been lifted off its moorings by heavy rainfall and had floated downriver just a couple of months after it opened in 1858. The Melan Bridge lasted a little longer — 68 years, to be exact — before two spans collapsed and plunged into the water, killing a driver whose car was thrown into the high water below. A new bridge, which opened two years later, was already under construction when two of the Melan Bridge's five main spans failed.

Other bridges, fortunately, proved more durable, such as the open-spandrel concrete arch bridge in southern Virginia, pictured below. It's still in use today and coming up on a century old.

The concrete-arch Smith River Bridge on U.S. Highway 58 in Martinsville, Va., opened in 1927 and was typical of the style used during the period. It replaced a covered bridge that was built on the stone pillars seen in the foreground.

Right: The closed Arroyo Hondo Bridge parallels the modern alignment of U.S. 101 in Santa Barbara County along the Central California coast. Built in 2018, it's more than 100 years old and was bypassed in 1984. The modern highway can be seen in the background. A railroad trestle is unseen at left.

Below: A newer (1955) open-spandrel bridge was built on U.S. 99 in Dunsmuir, Calif.; it's now part of Interstate 5.

YESTERDAY'S HIGHWAYS

Above: Two bridges carry Main Street traffic in Danville, Va., across the Dan River. The one at right was built in 1927, while its companion span was replaced with a new bridge in 2005.

Right: The view from under the 2005 bridge, with the 1927 bridge in background at far right.

The Lincoln Highway Columbia-Wrightsville Bridge spans the Susquehanna River between Lancaster and York counties in Pennsylvania. Dedicated in 1930, it's the world's longest concrete multiple-arch bridge, with 48 total spans covering 6,657 feet.

Signed, Sealed and Delivered

Highway signs have evolved a bit over the years. During the first quarter of the 20th century, drivers were hit with a barrage of auto trail markers, posted on some 250 roads of varying quality by private "associations." But that began to change with legislation, passed in 1921, to put the federal government at the forefront of funding — and decision making — when it came to the nation's roads.

More specifically, its highways.

The funding formula approved in 1921 might have been called the 7% solution. Under that formula, federal funds could only be used on 7% of the nation's roads... three-sevenths of which (42%) *had to be* "interstate in character." According to another provision in the law, as much as 60% of the federal funds to be allocated — $75 million a year — could be spent those interstate roadways.

Or a cool $45 million, concentrated on 3% of U.S. roads.

The nation's highways were about to get a lot better, a lot faster, thanks to a huge infusion of cold, hard cash. That $75 million wasn't just for one year, either. The same amount would be spent annually throughout the 1920s.

With all that money came great power — power that had, heretofore, resided with the wealthy private sponsors of the auto trails. Suddenly, these businessmen were no longer in charge of how the money would be spent. Or, more to the point, *where* it would be spent. The government might well choose to improve roads that didn't parallel the Dixie Highway or the Lee Highway or the Lincoln Highway. It might choose more direct routes that bypassed the cities and towns the auto trail barons had chosen, for their own business reasons, to serve.

When it became clear that the government was about to use this new power to create a system of federal highways, cities and the businesses they served began lobbying in earnest to be sure they got a piece of the action.

It was 1925 when a panel of three federal and 21 state highway officials sat down to identify the nation's main roads. They knew they had quite a job ahead of them, so in some ways, they opted to start from scratch, holding a series of six meetings in an attempt to come up with the most reasonable system possible.

But "reasonable" didn't necessarily mean popular.

The board members decided to avoid holding public hearings for fear of attracting throngs of competing interests. Each, they knew, would be clamoring for a spot along one of the numbered routes the committee planned to designate. As the president of the American Association of State Highway Officials put it: "As soon as the purpose and work of the proposed board shall become known, the infernal regions will begin popping." Translation: Everyone with a stake in the committee's decision was bound to be up in arms.

One decision that was bound to be controversial: The panel chose *not* to consider the current state of any road as a factor for inclusion in the national network. In other words, the road could be in pretty bad shape, as long as it appeared to be the best way to get from one place to another. It could always be improved; that's where the federal funding came in.

The existing trails, in any case, were a hot mess. In seeking to serve as many businesses as possible, one trail offered alternate alignments over three separate roads. (Note the Dixie Highway's many permutations, left.) The upshot, according to one assessment: "Most routes followed their financial support, and it was impossible to integrate many of them into any logical highway system."

YESTERDAY'S HIGHWAYS

The committee had its work cut out for it, considering the sheer number of auto trails zigzagging across the country. One road, for example, carried eight different trail makers for a fair distance. In another case, 70% of one trail overlapped with other marked routes. And there was a trail that overlapped with up to 11 others.

The factors that were taken into account when trying to sort out this chaotic jumble?

- County population figures.
- The value of agricultural produce, in dollars, for those counties.
- The value of counties' manufacturing, mineral and forest products

The panel started out with a uniform set of maps provided by the Post Office and charted the results to determine which routes would serve the most people, and their economic interests, most effectively. Once the committee had hammered out a plan that included some 75,000 miles of road, it unveiled the proposed system to the states… which immediately sought changes, most of them at the behest of trail associations. The panel then made 142 adjustments, increasing the mileage substantially to nearly 97,000. This was the plan ratified by the states.

To help motorists keep things straight, even numbers were assigned to east-west highways, with odd numbers reserved for north-south roads. The number of overlapping highways was reduced, but not eliminated. For instance, one stretch of highway in Southern California was signed as U.S. 99, 70 and 60. How could "even" and "odd" highways share the same road? Highway 99 was primarily a north-south highway, but in this area, it ran east to west. (The discrepancy was later eliminated when the interstate system laid out I-10 over the same route.) Some signs in California's San Fernando Valley referred to U.S. 101 "north" even where the road ran east and west; other signs, however, referred to U.S. 101 "west."

The look of those signs was decided, as well: They would take the form of cut-out shields, with black lettering on a white background. At first, the committee wanted to put the initials "U.S.A." at the top, but decided instead to place the state name in that position, with a black bar below it, and the initials "U.S." in the main field, just above the route number.

Over the years, some states would experiment with variations, such as colored signs for different routes (in Florida) and different directions (in Arizona). And the federal standard would change, as well. In 1948, the original blocky typeface was dropped in favor of a smoother, curved font. In 1961, the black crossbar and all the lettering were eliminated except for the route number, which was still cast against a white shield but now set against a square, black background. That format was changed slightly in 1970, with slightly wider numbers.

California retained the old cutout style.

"Historic" rectangular signs with the white shield against a brown background can now be seen along some stretches of retired federal highways, such as 99 and 66.

A U.S. 58 sign along the Jeb Stuart Highway in southern Virginia.

YESTERDAY'S HIGHWAYS

Clockwise from top: A highway junction in Waco, Texas, photographed by Lee Russell in 1939; a man with proposed road signs in 1925, the year before the federal highway system was inaugurated; another sign in Waco from Russell's camera. *Library of Congress photos*

Left: Sign at the southern end of old U.S. 99 at the Mexican border.

Below: A historic U.S. 66 sign in Carlinville, Ill. marks an alignment used from 1926 to 1930.

YESTERDAY'S HIGHWAYS

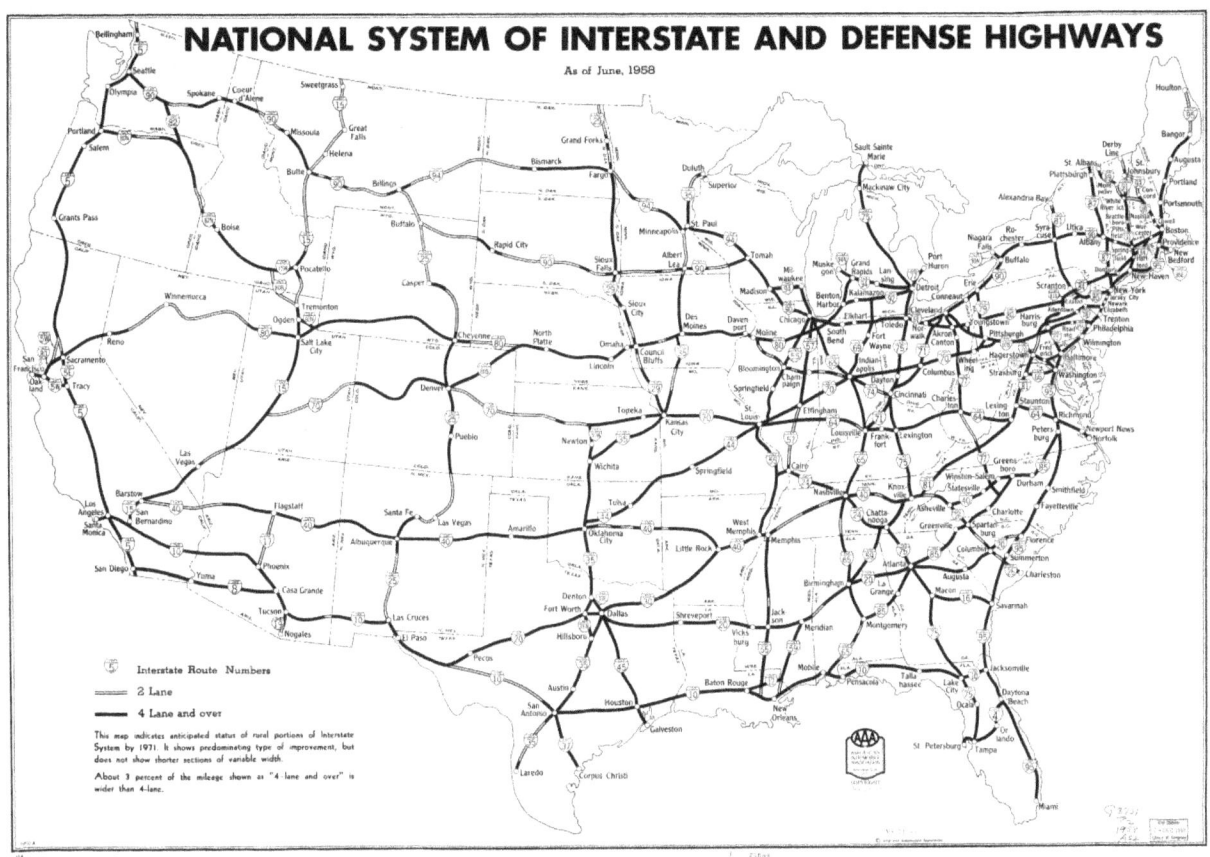

President Eisenhower inaugurated a new era when he signed the Federal Highway Act of 1956, authorizing the creation of a $114 billion Interstate Highway System. The concept had been in the works since the late '30s, when a feasibility study focused on the idea of six toll-road superhighways — three running north and south, and three more running east and west.

The toll-road idea was never implemented, and the proposal soon grew to encompass an entire network of interstate highways. In 1941, President Franklin Roosevelt appointed a committee to study a full-scale national expressway system. It turned in its report three years later, calling for 33,900 miles of "interregional highways" and 5,000 miles of urban auxiliary routes.

The bill signed by Eisenhower expanded on this further, identifying 41,000 miles of highway.

The roads would be required to have:

- At least two lanes in each direction.
- Lanes that were 12 feet wide, with 10 feet of paved shoulder on the right and 4 feet on the left.
- Limited access, via on- and off-ramps rather than cross streets.

The design was meant to accommodate traffic levels 20 years into the future — and serve as a conduit for military transport in times of national emergency.

New shields were designed: White numerals were set against a blue background on a main field that also included the state's name in smaller letters; this field was topped by a red strip with white letters spelling out "INTERSTATE."

(Business loops and spurs are marked by green shields with white lettering.)

As with the old federal highway system, north-south roads received odd numbers, with even numbers reserved for interstates running east and west. Major highways had one- or two-digit numbers, with three-digit variations being used for beltways, spurs and urban freeways. In the Los Angeles area, interstates 110, 210 and 710 were designed as spurs of the main east-west freeway, I-10. Meanwhile, interstates 405 and 605 were created as spurs of the primary north-south thoroughfare, Interstate 5 (as was I-805 in San Diego).

Some of the new interstates paralleled older federal highways, relegating them to second-class status — much to the chagrin of businesses owners along those older roads. Iconic numbers such as Route 66 weren't duplicated under the new system, either.

U.S. 99 ceased to exist as a federal highway in California when I-5 was built along the west side of the San Joaquin Valley. The road itself was still there, but it was no longer funded by the federal government: Henceforth, the state would be called upon to maintain it. Green California "spade" shields went up, replacing the black-on-white federal shields to mark the transition. (U.S. 101, by contrast, retained its federal status.)

Interstate 40 ran alongside Route 66 through the Southwest from Oklahoma to Arizona, reducing businesses and even entire towns along the old road to ghosts. Interstate 80 ran parallel to the Lincoln Highway (U.S. 30) across much of the Plains. Interstate 81 followed U.S. 11 and the old Great Valley Road through Virginia.

The more things stayed the same… the more they changed.

Service Stations

This Shell station was one of eight built during the 1920s in Winston-Salem, N.C., and is the only one to survive today.

All Pumped Up

The first gas station was built in 1905 in St. Louis, followed by a second two years later in Seattle; Gulf opened the first drive-in station in Pittsburgh a few weeks before Christmas in 1913.

By 1919, A.L. Westgard wrote in *The Independent*, "repair shops and supply stations" were "everywhere at convenient intervals on all the standard routes." There was no longer any need for motorists to carry gasoline or spare parts with them, he remarked (although they might want to take along a canteen of water if they were traveling in the West).

Before the era of the modern service station, motorists had to fuel up at places like Kearfott's Drug Store in Martinsville, Va. When eight cars rumbled through the southern Virginia town on the 1906 Glidden Tour from New York to Jacksonville, they had only two options when it came to buying gas: Kearfott's or the newly opened Hairston & Townes Garage. There weren't any driveways or gas pumps: Gasoline would be delivered curbside in gallon jugs, and motorists carried spare cans sealed with a potato on the spout (yes, a potato!) to keep dirt from contaminating the gas.

The Gulf station in Pittsburgh changed the game. Drivers could pull in off the street via a concrete driveway that branched out to either side of a modest building. The octagonal brick station resembled a Chinese pagoda — or, perhaps, a mushroom. Gulf sold 30 gallons of gas on its first day of business at 27 cents a gallon and was soon building other stations in the area, as seen in the 1914 ad below.

The genie was out of the bottle.

YESTERDAY'S HIGHWAYS

Early on, the oil industry was divided into two groups: Companies that were descended from Standard Oil and those that weren't. Standard, founded by John D. Rockefeller in 1870, used its clout to all but corner the market on the oil industry before the automobile was even invented. Rockefeller negotiated sweetheart shipping deals with railroad companies that allowed him to undersell his competitors, then bought those competitors when they couldn't match his prices.

By 1904, Standard controlled 91% of oil production and 85% of sales nationwide. Since the auto industry was still in its infancy, most of what it produced was kerosene.

That, however, would soon change.

As cars became more common, the focus would switch to gasoline and motor oil (Pennzoil, for example, was originally part of the Standard conglomerate). In 1906, Standard's market share was down to 70%, as companies like Gulf and Texaco began breaking into the field. But that didn't stop the federal government from suing Standard under the Sherman Antitrust Act, charging that it had become a monopoly and needed to be "broken up."

The government won its case in 1911 when the Supreme Court ruled that Standard Oil should be split into 34 companies — most of them oil or pipeline firms. Foremost them were the so-called "seven sisters" and two other companies that would become major players over the course of the next century: Atlantic and Conoco.

Company	Name	Modern status
Atlantic	Atlantic	Arco (Richfield merger)
Continental Oil	Conoco	ConocoPhillips (Phillips merger)
Ohio Oil Company	Marathon	Marathon
Standard Oil of California	Chevron	Chevron
Standard Oil of Indiana	Amoco	Acquired by BP
Standard Oil of Kentucky	Kyso	Acquired by Chevron
Standard Oil of New Jersey	Esso	Exxon (merged with Mobil)
Standard Oil of New York	Socony	Mobil (merged with Exxon)
Standard Oil (Ohio)	Sohio	Acquired by BP

Several smaller oil companies also rose from the ashes of the Standard monolith. But despite the antitrust case, a number of them wound up being purchased by other, larger survivors of the breakup. Amoco bought three of them: Standard of Illinois, Kansas and Minnesota. Chevron gobbled up a fourth, Standard of Iowa.

Meanwhile, other companies had begun to emerge. Gulf, as mentioned, built the first drive-in service station. Texaco, founded as The Texas Company, was notable as the first to have presence in each of the lower 48 states, or "clear across the nation," as its ads proclaimed.

The following table shows a few of big players.

Company	Founded		Developments
Associated	1901	California	Acquired by Phillips, 1966*
Cities Gas	1910	Oklahoma	Branded as Citgo
Gilmore	1903	California	Acquired by Mobil, 1945
Gulf	1901	Pennsylvania	Acquired by Chevron, 1985
Humble	1911	Texas	Acquired by Esso (Exxon), 1959
Phillips	1917	Oklahoma	Merged with Conoco, 2002
Pure	1914	New Jersey	Acquired by Union Oil, 1965**
Richfield	1905	California	Merged with Atlantic, 1966***
Royal Dutch Shell	1907	England	Shell
Sinclair	1916	New York	Sinclair****
Sun Oil	1886	Pennsylvania	Sunoco
Texaco	1901	Texas	Merged with Chevron, 2001
Tidewater (Tydol)	1887	New York	Merged with Associated, 1938
Union 76 (Unocal)	1890	California	Merged with Chevron, 2005

* Merged with Tydol in 1938; products sold at Flying A stations
** Name revived in 1993, now based in South Carolina
*** This merger formed ARCO, later purchased by BP
**** Acquired by ARCO in 1969; sold to Robert (Earl) Holding, 1976

YESTERDAY'S HIGHWAYS

Gulf started the trend of branded service stations (also known as filling stations), and other companies quickly joined the fray. Service stations came in all shapes and sizes. Some looked like little cottages, others like colonial homes; some were simple metal boxes, others were almost palatial. An early trend was to make stations look residential, so they'd be convenient to neighborhood residents without being eyesores. The idea was to make them "fit right in."

One such design was adopted by Pure Oil in 1925. It featured a steeply gabled roof with a chimney on a tiny house that looked almost fit for a gnome. There weren't any service bays or mechanics on duty; just a homey design that even featured a false chimney out front — adorned with the letter "P" for the company name.

The photo below shows a station along Route 66 in McLean, Texas, that also uses a "P" on the chimney but has been restored as a Phillips Petroleum station, which is a different company entirely.

Indeed, Pure wasn't the only company to adopt the cottage look early on, as the following pages show.

Right: Another former Pure Oil station, on Main Street (State Route 57) in Danville, Va., includes a garage in its architecture.

Below: A DX station on Illinois State Route 146 in Calconda also features a gabled roof and residential look.

YESTERDAY'S HIGHWAYS

Two more stations with the cottage look can be seen in Sutherland, Neb., along the Lincoln Highway. **Top:** An old gabled Phillips 66 station from around the 1930s utilized the chain's Cotswold design; it had been converted into a sweet shop as of 2019, with the front door replacing the old garage. **Above:** A simpler Frontier station from c. 1927 has been restored.

Stations near the urban core were, naturally, more constrained by space limitations and tended to look more "boxed in" than their suburban counterparts.

Urban stations, clockwise from top: Dunkle's in Bedford, Pa., which opened in 1933; the first station in Minerva, Ohio; and a former Cities Service stop in Webb City, Mo., that's been converted into a Route 66 center.

YESTERDAY'S HIGHWAYS

As time went on, gas stops grew elaborate. "Cottages" began to look more like full-fledged homes, augmented by garages where repair work could be done. Sinclair added the first three stations with lubrication equipment in 1926. On the East Coast particularly, colonial-style architecture became popular, with some stations exchanging faux chimneys for decorative cupolas.

A pair of Mid-Atlantic examples can be seen below: a station in the Washington, D.C., area, directly below, and a former Sunoco station, at bottom, that has been converted into a restaurant called the Third Bay Café in Martinsville, Va.

The architecture out west, in the nation's heartland, took a variety of different turns. On Route 66, the Ambler-Becker Texaco station in Dwight, Okla., below, looked pretty much like any other house — with the exception of the pump island out front. It opened in 1933 and operated longer than any other station along the Mother Road, serving motorists for 66 years without interruption before it closed in 1999.

Sprague's Super Service, at bottom, opened in 1931 in a Tudor-style building that also included a café and garage, in addition to apartments on the second story for the owner and station attendant. The station in Normal, Ill., stopped dispensing gasoline four decades after it opened.

YESTERDAY'S HIGHWAYS

Sprague's was an independent station, but as more miles of roadway were laid down and more cars headed for the open road, service station chains with grand visions began to dot the landscape.

One of the most ambitious projects was undertaken by Richfield on the West Coast in the late 1920s: a series of more than 30 stations, mostly up and down the main north-south U.S. highways (99 and 101) that would go far beyond the limited idea of simple gas stops. Many would also include a café and "tavern" — not an Irish pub, but actually a motor inn.

Stations in Southern and Central California would be built in Spanish mission style; those in the Pacific Northwest would resemble Swiss chalets. But the crowning touch at each site would be its beacon tower: a steel structure that looked something like an oil derrick, only taller and narrower. Each would rise 125 feet above the highway and be topped with a directional beacon that glowed with 8 million candlepower, making it visible for miles around.

A Beacon tower in Willows, Calif., one of two still standing as of 2019 (the other is in Mt. Shasta, to the north).

Visible to whom?

The beacons had two intended audiences. First, they were designed for the highway motorist looking for the next opportunity to fill up or bed down for the night. The beacons were placed strategically every 50 miles or so, making it convenient for drivers to plan regular stops along the way. Second, they were meant to be visible to aircraft flying overhead: Pilots could use them to stay on course as they flew up and down the coast in an era before radar.

The first six beacons lit up on Dec. 17, 1928 — all of them in California: Palm City, Beaumont, Capistrano, Livermore, Merced and Santa Rosa. Beacons in Castaic, El Centro and Visalia joined them within a couple of months.

A Richfield Beacon station still stands in front of a shopping center along U.S. 101 in Paso Robles, Calif. The interior of the structure has been closed, and the building stands at what is now a bus stop.

Beacon opened its first café and 50-room "tavern" on Route 66 in Barstow. Like many of the beacons, it was built near an airport, and it opened with a fiesta celebration on June 27, 1930. But by that time, the overall project was already doomed to failure. The advent of the Great Depression put a financial strain on Richfield, which would eventually declare bankruptcy, and forced it to abandon the effort before it could be completed.

No more inns or cafés would be built (although plans for Visalia, Santa Maria and San Juan Capistrano had been announced), and four pieces of property intended for beacon stations remained vacant. Richfield emerged from bankruptcy with a new owner, and the Depression finally came to an end, but by that time, pilots found their way from place to place with the help of radar and no longer had any need for bright and shining visual aids.

Suddenly obsolete, the beacons started coming down. Barstow's tower served as a sign for a bowling alley for several years before being torn down in 1970, with the Paso Robles tower on U.S. 101 being dismantled in 1995. That left just two towers standing — in Willows and Mt. Shasta. Richfield, meanwhile, went on to merge with Atlantic Oil, forming ARCO in 1966. (For a more detailed discussion of Richfield Beacon history, see my book *Highway 99: The History of California's Main Street*.)

YESTERDAY'S HIGHWAYS

Remnants of Richfield, from top: The Richfield eagle on a restored pump on old U.S. 101 in San Miguel; an abandoned Richfield station, with faded lettering on the side, along California State Route 41 in Easton, south of Fresno; a restored Richfield station in Coalinga dating from 1933 on California State Route 33.

Above: An old-style Phillips 66 sign outside the Spencer Garage along a concrete section of Route 66 in Spencer, Mo. The black-and-orange logo was in use from 1930 until 1959.

Left: A newer-style Phillips 66 sign along Route 66 in St. James, Mo.

While Richfield was staking out a presence along the West Coast's two main federal highways, 99 and 101, two other companies were making themselves fixtures on Route 66. One of them — Phillips 66 — even incorporated that route number into its name. The company was based in Bartlesville, Okla., but its refinery was just off Route 66.

YESTERDAY'S HIGHWAYS

The first Phillips first station, which opened in 1927, wasn't along the Mother Road, but in Wichita, Kansas. Still, it wasn't long before stations started popping up along the famed highway, with the company even adopting an orange-and-black variation on the highway's iconic shield as its official logo in 1930.

By this time, major chains had already begun putting the "service" in "service station." National Supply Stations of Los Angeles, bought out by Chevron in 1914, started the trend when it trotted out gas station attendants in white uniforms and black bow ties. Other chains, such as Shell, Gulf and Texaco, followed suit.

Even more than today, clean restrooms were a big deal. So, in the 1930s, Texaco hired a "White Patrol" to go from station to station and ensure the company's "Registered Rest Rooms" were clean. But Phillips went one step further: It hired "Highway Hostesses" to conduct surprise inspections at 66 stations, giving their seal of approval to restrooms that were fully stocked and squeaky clean. (In an interesting twist, Phillips only hired registered nurses for the job.)

A closed Phillips 66 station at the midway point on Route 66. The station is part of the Bent Door Café (the door is seen at right). A station first opened at the location in 1937, and was rebuilt in 1948 after a fire as Tommy's Café.

A restored Whiting Bros. gas sign stands vigil beside Route 66 in Moriarty, N.M.

The other major gas-station operator on Route 66 was a chain called Whiting Bros. Unlike Phillips, it's no longer in business today, but during the heyday of the Mother Road, its stations were ubiquitous along the western half of the route: At the chain's zenith, there were somewhere between 180 and 200 stations in the Southwest, many of them on 66 between Shamrock, Texas, and California.

The four Whiting brothers started out in a different business altogether. Their father owned a lumber mill, and they began selling gasoline by the can in 1917 in St. Johns, Ariz. When the federal government chose a section of the National Old Trails Road to become part of Route 66 from New Mexico west to the Pacific, the Whitings saw an opportunity to cash in. They moved their base of operations northwest to Holbrook, Ariz., along the new highway and used lumber from their father's mill to build a cheap service station.

Their ability to keep costs low was key to their rapid success, as they expanded quickly to other locations in Arizona, including Winslow and Flagstaff. Stations in

YESTERDAY'S HIGHWAYS

Colorado, Utah (as far north as Provo) and south to the Mexican border followed, with the chain reaching a total of 100 by 1965. Like Richfield with its chain of beacons, the Whiting Bros. aimed to expand beyond gasoline service, offering groceries and overnight accommodations at many of their sites.

Whiting Bros. set up billboards along the roadside to signal motorists that they were approaching a station, and the stations themselves were hard to miss. Large signs towered above the side of the highway in bright red and yellow, standing out against the desert bluffs and plains. The brothers originally sold Pathfinder brand gasoline but later, in the 1960s, partnered with Phillips to sell its petroleum and diesel.

Whiting Bros. offered a number of incentives and promotions in addition to its regular low prices. Many stations were open 24 hours, and the company gave away free road maps to all who asked, even if they didn't make a purchase. Whiting offered a "courtesy card" that repeat customers could present to receive a special price "except when a credit card is used or a local Price War is in effect." Another incentive in 1960 was a giveaway that offered the chance to win a Ford Falcon or one of 1,000 other "tremendous prizes."

When Interstate 40 bypassed Route 66, directing traffic away from the stations, they started to close, with the last of them being sold off in the 1990s. Most of the old buildings have been torn down or repurposed, but a few original signs and buildings remain along old Route 66.

A Whiting Bros. sign still bears the company's simple slogan, "Gas for Less," on Route 66 in Winslow, Ariz.

Surviving Whiting Bros. signs along Route 66 in San Fidel, N.M. (top, right) and Moriarty, N.M. (above).

YESTERDAY'S HIGHWAYS

Top: The restored Whiting Bros. station in Moriarty, N.M. **Above and right:** An old Whiting Bros. station and its sign in Amarillo, Texas.

Clockwise from above left: Former Whiting Bros. stations in San Fidel, N.M.; Truxton, Ariz.; and Bagdad, Calif.

YESTERDAY'S HIGHWAYS

A number of old Whiting Bros. stations remain along Route 66, although many are barely recognizable today. **Top:** A station in Holbrook, Ariz., retains a faded stripe from the days it operated. **Above**: An ad for another company adorns the canopy of a former Whiting Bros. station in Continental Divide, N.M.

Oil Company Slogans

Atlantic Oil	*Atlantic Keeps Your Car on the Go*
Citgo	*Fueling Good*
Esso / Enco	*A Smile for Every Mile*
	Happy Motoring
	Put a Tiger in Your Tank
Flying A / Associated	*Flying A Puts Wings on Your Car*
	Let's Get Associated
Gilmore	*Roar with Gilmore*
Gulf	*That Good Gulf Gasoline*
Marathon	*Best in the Long Run*
Mobil	*At the Sign of the Flying Red Horse*
Phillips 66	*Phill Up with Phillips*
	The Gasoline that Won the West
Pure	*Be Sure with Pure*
Shell	*Service is Our Business*
	You Can Be Sure with Shell
Signal	*The Go Farther Gasoline*
Sinclair	*Drive with Care and Buy Sinclair*
Sunoco	*Stop at Sunoco... Go with Confidence!*
Texaco	*Wherever You Go... Trust Texaco*
	You Can Trust Your Car to the Man Who Wears the Star
Union 76	*Go with the Spirit... the Spirit of 76*
Whiting Bros.	*Quality Gas for Less*

YESTERDAY'S HIGHWAYS

A restored Gilmore gas station at the Los Angeles Farmers Market spotlights the lion logo and the company's reputation for winning races.

In the 1920s, oil companies started adding tetraethyl lead, or "Ethyl," which eliminated an annoying "knocking" sound and reduced wear on engine valves. Many stations offered two alternatives: regular and the pricier Ethyl. But it still was hard to distinguish one gas brand from another. In practical terms, companies could tout their products' use in winning race cars or record-setting speed endeavors, but why stop there? It was much more helpful if drivers could actually see the difference.

To this end, Los Angeles-based Gilmore became the first company to introduce color to its gasoline. In the 1920s, gas was dispensed from pumps with glass globes at the top, so motorists could actually see the fuel inside. Gilmore added coloring to its product and marketed it as "Blu-Green" gas: The color didn't improve performance, but it did make the gasoline *look* distinctive.

Gilmore also boosted publicity by hiring a pilot named Roscoe Turner to fly around with a lion cub — named Gilmore, naturally — in a company-branded airplane during the 1930s. (Gilmore's mascot was a lion, and its slogan invited motorists to "Roar with Gilmore"). Later, in 1948, the company not only built football and baseball stadiums, but also opened one of the first self-service stations, which it called a "Gas-a-Teria."

"Dino," right, stands watch outside a Sinclair station in Nebraska. Sinclair was founded in 1916 by Henry Sinclair even floated a balloon version of its famed mascot in the Macy's Thanksgiving Day Parade.

Gilmore had its lion, but Sinclair came up with an even more memorable mascot: a brontosaurus, which made its debut during the 1933-34 World's Fair in Chicago. The company showcased a 70-foot version of "Dino" alongside some prehistoric pals (a T-rex, stegosaurus, triceratops and hadrosaur) in a Dinoland Pavilion six years later when the event was held at New York.

Many stations lured drivers with products and freebies that had nothing to do with gas. Trading stamps such as S&H Green Stamps became a staple: Stations gave out stamps with every purchase, which could be redeemed for products in the S&H catalog.

Other giveaways ranged from the practical to the kitschy. Sinclair (naturally) put out dinosaurs: plush dinosaurs, plastic dinosaurs, dino-shaped soap and even dinosaur stamps. The stamps were issued weekly at stations starting in 1935 that could be affixed to albums provided by the company. By the end of the promotion, Sinclair had distributed 4 million albums and 48 million stamps.

The stamps weren't the only "collect 'em all" promotional sets issued by gas stations.

YESTERDAY'S HIGHWAYS

In 1969, Shell issued a set of 31 presidential coins that could be redeemed for prizes when you filled up all the spaces on a collector's card. If you were lucky enough to get a James Madison coin, you could redeem it for $1,000, and Martin Van Buren was worth $500.

Union 76 came up with a real trend-setter in 1967 when it produced the world's first antenna-topping ball in the shape of its iconic globe sign. Many of the spheres atop the Union signs would rotate slowly, drawing the eyes of passing motorists; some later versions of the sign were circular but flat or with a slight bulge, such as the one at right, at an abandoned station in Valentine, Ariz., on Route 66.

Road maps were a staple, while free glasses, cups, dinnerware and even steak knives were common incentives, but kitsch for kids was particularly popular. In 1969, Gulf gave away free lunar module kits: sheets of cardboard with pieces that could be punched out, folded and assembled to

create a model of the Apollo 11 lander. Two years later, ARCO riffed on its company name by giving away a Noah's Ark set with pairs of plastic gorillas, alligators, hippos, lions and so forth. The animals were definitely not to scale: The skunks and aardvarks were as large as the elephants.

When Flying A stations adopted a cute but sad-looking Basset hound named Axelrod as the face of its "Ooooh, do we worry" ad campaign, it produced piggy banks (doggy banks?) in his image, as well as stuffed dogs and other collectibles for the kids to spread the word.

Meanwhile, the stations themselves continued to evolve.

Their numbers rose dramatically in the 1920s, from 15,000 at the beginning of the decade to nearly 124,000 at the dawn of the Great Depression. That rate of growth outpaced the increase in the number cars on the road, even though that figure, too, rose dramatically: from just over 9 million in 1920 to more than 26 million a decade later.

In the 1930s, companies increasingly moved away from residential locations and onto the open highway. With this shift came a move away from the "cottage" style that had been designed to blend into neighborhoods and toward what was then a more "modern" Art Deco look. These stations featured rounded corners and a sleeker yet classic feel, emblemized by the Conoco Tower at the U-Drop Inn, below, a 1936 station on Route 66 at U.S. 83 in Shamrock, Texas. (The name "U-Drop Inn" was chosen in a contest, with an 8-year-old boy winning $50 for his entry.)

A former gas station on Higuera Street (old U.S. 101) in San Luis Obispo, Calif., shows the Art Deco style with its rounded corners and smooth lines.

A castle-style Standard station stands on Illinois State Route 146 in Vienna, Ill. Built c. 1930, it was one of several in this style built across the country.

Ever since the first gas station opened in Pittsburgh, stations have tried to make it a little less uncomfortable for motorists to fill up in harsh weather. Whether you're pumping gas in the Northeast snow or in the scorching heat of the desert Southwest, you appreciate a little shelter from the elements. Stations sought to provide that with canopies over their pump islands. The canopies were sometimes modest, and sometimes expansive to the point of looking like flying wings.

Canopies, top to bottom: Jess Sours Garage, on old U.S. 29 in Virginia; and stations on Route 66 in eastern Oklahoma and eastern California.

Some canopies, such as the one on the 1930 Magnolia station in Texola, Oklahoma, **top**, have been attached to or extended from the main building; others, such as the crooked one **above** on Route 66 north of St. Louis, were built separately from the station.

Two examples of canopies incorporated into the structure of stations. **Top:** a former gas station on old California State Route 1 at the south end of Cambria became a bead shop for a quarter-century. **Above:** The Shady Bend Gas Station, Grocery and Diner opened in 1931 on the Lincoln Highway in Grand Island, Neb.

Sometimes, a canopy is more than just a canopy. A World War II fighter plane appears to have crashed into this circular canopy at the Quik Stop Mini Mart on old California State Route 41 (Elm Avenue) south of Fresno. It was known as AirGas when it opened in the 1950s.

Gas Stations in Decline

Many gas stations have pulled out their pumps and shut their doors in recent years.

The decline of the American service station as an institution began with the advent of widespread self-service in the 1970s. A few stations, such as the Gilmore Gas-a-Teria, had experimented with the concept, but full service remained the rule of the day. Then, in 1964, an inventor named Herb Timms made a breakthrough: He developed a box that would allow an attendant to activate gas pumps remotely. Suddenly, the employee no longer had to meet the driver at the pump to dispense gas. He could just flip a switch behind the counter. That system was first used in Westminster, Colo.

Still, the number of stations continued to climb, reaching its zenith at more than 216,000 in 1970. That was more than three years before the Arab oil embargo sent prices soaring and helped change the nature the American service station. Costs soared, and California passed a law that required all stations to post their prices — placing an emphasis on value over service.

It would hard to overstate the magnitude of this shift. Once upon a time, service stations really *were* about service. It was a way to get a leg up on the competition. In 1954, for instance, one Sinclair station ran an ad that specifically asked, "How much <u>service</u> per gallon of gas?" (The word really was underlined in the ad.)

Then, it answered its own question:

"It depends on where you buy your gasoline." The ad asserted that "the success of our business depends a great deal on the service we provide and the manner in which we perform it." That's why you could depend on receiving free, "helpful service, as well as for high-quality Sinclair Products ... whenever you (saw) the Sinclair Sign":

- Battery inspection
- Tire check
- Radiator check
- Air filter check
- Fan belt check
- Oil level check
- Windshield cleaned

- Wiper blades cleaned
- Rear window cleaned

Modern drivers head to a lube and oil center for this kind of assistance (usually after seeing their check-engine light go on). But once upon a time, you could count on your local service station to supply all these things.

And it wasn't just Sinclair. Other stations offered the same kind of service from uniformed attendants — who responded the sound of a bell triggered whenever a car pulled into the station. Chevron offered a "service pledge" in a series of ads that ran in 1954 across the western United States:

In some ways, service stations were behind the curve. Self-service in other retail industries had begun to take hold in the 1950s with the advent of discount stores — a trend that accelerated with the appearance of superstores such as Kmart, Target and Walmart in the early '60s. One of the main ways discounters trimmed prices was by cutting back on service. They eliminated department desks and invited customers to push shopping carts and check out at the front of the store. They didn't hire tailors, doormen, elevator operators or shoe salesmen.

In a sense, gas station attendants were just the latest casualty of this trend.

In the 1970s, self-service spread across the United States. Only New Jersey and

Oregon held out, standing firmly in the full-service camp by banning self-serve stations. Overall, however, as service declined, so did the number of gas stations: from 216,000 in 1970 to fewer than 159,000 a decade later and just 111,000 by the time 1990 rolled around.

Gas stations also closed as more freeways bypassed downtowns and city centers, where cars had been forced to stop at red lights and stop signs. Now, instead, they zipped by on interstates. Motorists passing through Martinsville, Va., on Church Street in 1940 could choose among three stations in just a little more than two blocks; none exist there today. And the same story can be told for uncounted cities and towns across the country.

Still more gas stations shut their doors as other retailers, such as supermarkets, big-box discount stores and mini-marts got into the business of selling gas.

What happened to those stations once they closed?

A survey of the American landscape provides a variety of answers. The Pacific Coast Highway once ran through Cambria, California, but when a modern bypass replaced that old alignment, it left Main Street to local and tourist traffic: You didn't have to go *through* town to get *past* town.

One Cambria station became a bead shop, another former station became a bakery, and a third was converted into a restaurant.

An old gas station on the Lincoln Highway in Van Wert, Ohio, has been repurposed as a pizza place.

YESTERDAY'S HIGHWAYS

A 1935 Gilmore station in Hollywood reopened as a Starbucks drive-up coffee shop. A station in Republic, Mo., became an architect's office. One in Smithfield, Utah became an insurance office. A Delhart, Texas, station was transformed into a salon. A bicycle shop; a pawn shop; an auto repair shop; a florist — these were just some of the new uses found for former service stations.

Not all service stations were repurposed, though. Converting a station to a new use can be complicated, not to mention expensive. Architectural changes may be needed. Environmental work may be required. In the case of the old Gilmore station, a large-scale cleanup project was needed, because large amounts of oil had leaked into the soil over the years. With so many gas stations being shuttered, it's no surprise that, in many cases, it just wasn't worth it. As a result, large numbers of abandoned and decaying stations litter the landscape across the country.

An old station in Glenrio, Texas, appears on the verge of falling down. Glenrio was founded at the dawn of the 20th century on the Texas-New Mexico state line and became a popular stop along Route 66. But when the Main Street of America was bypassed by Interstate 40, business dried up. The last two residents left sometime in the 1980s, making Glenrio a ghost town.

Clockwise from top: Abandoned gas stations along Route 66 in Glenrio, Texas; U.S. 101 — complete with ironic "OPEN" sign — north of Paso Robles, Calif.; and beside Route 66 south of Miami, Okla.

YESTERDAY'S HIGHWAYS

Clockwise from top left: Abandoned station on U.S. 66 in Afton, Okla.; a rusted sign along the Lincoln Highway; and a boarded-up station in Erick, Okla.

A fading Standard sign lies by the side of the road lies beside Route 66 west of Moriarty, N.M.

Some owners of properties still occupied by gas stations have decided to restore them to their former glory. Others have rebuilt lost stations from scratch, as with the station below: a re-creation of a 1930 Sinclair station on Route 66 at Paris Springs, Mo., that was rebuilt after fire destroyed it in 1955. Some former stations may house new businesses, tourist centers or museums, or they may just have been restored for a love of history. Whatever the reason, many still exist in various parts of the country.

YESTERDAY'S HIGHWAYS

Above: A 1930s Shell station in Fieldale, Va., has been converted into an antique shop by a retired journalist.

Left: A restored Kan-O-Tex station on Route 66, which opened in 1934, is now a souvenir shop.

Above: An old Signal box station has been maintained along U.S. 101 in Northern California. Such stations were cheap to produce and easy to set up (and tear down). **Below:** A restored Route 66 Texaco station in Tucumcari, N.M., with one of the town's many murals on the side.

YESTERDAY'S HIGHWAYS

Some photos from an age gone by...

From top: An impressive Gulf station photographed in Miami by Marion Post Walcott in 1939; Denham's Super Service Shell station advertised Quaker State motor oil when Lee Russell took this photograph in 1942, but the pumps appear to have been removed. *Library of Congress photos*

Top: The neon Richfield eagle was lit up during an overcast day in Redding, California, when Lee Russell took this photo in 1942. *Library of Congress*

Above: A Richfield station in Solano County, California, features mission-style architecture and heavy, rectangular columns holding up its canopy. Lee Russell snapped this picture in 1940. *Library of Congress*

YESTERDAY'S HIGHWAYS

Left: Full service was the rule of the day until the 1970s. Here, a uniformed gas station attendant equipped with a change counter fills up a motorist's Dodge at a Washington, D.C., Gulf station in 1942. *Albert Freeman, Library of Congress*

Above: A truck pulls up outside a Conoco station in Penasco, N.M., in this 1940 photo by Lee Russell. *Library of Congress*

From top: Country and city pumps provide a contrast in these two photos by Lee Russell, the first taken at a station in Edcouch, Texas, in 1939, and the second from Hollywood California three years later. *Library of Congress*

YESTERDAY'S HIGHWAYS

Truck Stops and Travel Centers

A big rig heads north on California State Route 86 near the Salton Sea.

Keep on Truckin'

It's hard to miss the big rigs, buses, tractor-trailers and the like that are so common on the modern highway. For years, highways have been the economic backbone of the regions they served, passing through fertile farmland and industrial centers, and traversing mountain passes.

Highway 99 in California is the perfect example: Grain silos, warehouses and distribution centers line the road, once a federal highway and now a part of the state road system.

In its heyday, before the government built Interstate 5 on the sparsely populated west side of the San Joaquin Valley, it didn't matter whether you were transporting raisins from Selma or dates from Indio: U.S. 99 was the way to go.

Still, even today, if you're behind the wheel of a Mercedes or a Mazda, you might not pay much attention to the infrastructure built around the trucking industry. The average motorist might cross the Tehachapi mountain range that divides Northern and Southern California without taking much notice of signs with messages such as "6% grade 2½ miles ahead" and "Trucks use low gears."

Trucks are supposed to observe a lower speed limit and keep to the right, so swifter automobiles can pass. Runaway truck ramps, with their heavy gravel to slow down out-of-control big rigs, are visible on downgrades of many highways. They're escape routes, giving trucks a way to pull off the highway in times of crisis.

One reason trucks can be so dangerous on a steep downhill slope is their weight. Big rigs can weigh up to 40 tons, compared to the typical car at only 2½ tons. Once they get going at highway speeds, they can require two-thirds more pavement to stop once the brakes are applied — if the brakes are working. That's part of the reason California requires trucks rated above a certain weight (currently 11,500 pounds) to stop at scales cleverly designated as "weigh stations."

The state recognized the need for scales early. By 1929, several states had passed laws restricting the size of loads carried by trucks traveling on certain highways. The Los Angeles County Motor Patrol had developed a portable system that could be used to weigh trucks on the spot, using four portable scales — one for each wheel. The four readings were added together to come up with the total load size.

A small, independent truck scale operation sits just before a Highway 99 onramp north of Fresno, Calif.

YESTERDAY'S HIGHWAYS

Permanent truck scales weren't far behind. In 1938, officials set up a 24-hour truck-checking station at Fort Tejon, near the point where the U.S. 99 began the steepest portion of its descent into the San Joaquin Valley. Highway Patrol officers were on hand to make sure loads were within limits defined under state law.

Private scales operated by companies such as CAT came later. The company opened its first scale in South Holland, Ill., in 1977 and had grown to 1,800 locations in North America by 2020.

Scales are far from the only highway business to have emerged in support of the trucking industry. As the nation shifted from the railroad to the highway as its primary means of transporting goods, a new industry sprang up to support the drivers who spent days away from home, driving long hours cross-country. They needed places to spend the night, to clean up, to grab some coffee and get a bite to eat. They also needed a place to buy the kind of fuel their semis ran on, diesel, which wasn't always available at traditional gas stations.

Truck stops sprang up to fill those needs.

Royal Truck Stop, off Interstate 10 in Colton, Calif.

Early truck stops were less elaborate than today's travel centers. **Top:** A trucker sticks his feet out of his passenger-side window in 1940 at a Washington, D.C., Truckers' Comfort Station on U.S. 1. **Above:** A truck stops in front of a Truckers Exchange Café and public scales in De Leon, Texas, a year earlier. *Library of Congress, photos by Jack Delano and Lee Russell*

A good night's sleep?

When it came to sleeping arrangements, truckers had to make do. Many roughed it by sleeping in their vehicles, whose wooden seats were anything but the epitome of comfort. Anything more elaborate was usually improvised, and not necessarily any more comfortable. One San Joaquin Valley-based company in California rigged up a couple of '22 Packards with wooden boxes over the cabs where the relief driver could sleep. (The casual observer might have feared an appearance by Dracula.)

By the mid-1930s, however, a few manufacturers had started offering sleepers as part of the package. The wooden boxes gave way to so-called "coffin sleepers," cramped quarters usually placed directly behind the cab. These compartments might have been 2 feet wide by 3 feet tall, giving the occupant barely enough room to turn over. Drivers with claustrophobic tendencies need not apply.

In the early 1950s, Kenworth offered a CBE model, which stood for "Cab-Beside-Engine." The CBE design included a sleeping space for the relief driver between the cab and the engine, a configuration that earned it the nickname "suicide sleeper": Few occupants could expect to survive a crash while they slept right next to the engine.

Some establishments that catered to travelers and tourists refused to serve truck drivers. But other stops offered various combinations of a garage, cheap accommodations and a diner or coffee shop that suited truckers pretty well. As time passed, some roadside establishments started catering specifically to truckers, seating them first at the lunch counter or offering them a place to shower in the back.

As trucks gained horsepower and load capacity, though, they outgrew "normal" highway stops designed for automobiles. Many early motor courts included carports alongside their cabins, but they were called CARports for a reason: They didn't provide enough clearance for trucks. Drivers ran into the same problem at some service stations, where canopies built to shield pumps from the elements were often too low to allow larger trucks access.

Flying A built a "flat-top" station off U.S. 99 in Fresno in 1952, which served motor vehicles of all shapes and sizes. It made sure truckers knew they were welcome, giving them their own entrance, access to diesel fuel and a 70-foot canopy that offered big rigs plenty of clearance. The station later became a Valero and was ultimately razed to make way for a high-speed rail project.

Truck stops offered an array of services that establishments catering to the auto traveler did not.

Many of the earliest among them, like the earliest motels and gas stations, were independent operations, but larger companies soon entered the fray once they realized they were missing a large segment of the market. Flying A's flat-top station in Fresno, with its 110-foot "GAS" tower on the west side of 99, was a prime example of an early truck stop. The canopy was 70 feet high, providing ample room for trucks — which got their own separate entrance. Diesel fuel was available; there was a "completely equipped" truck lube pit, a public scale capable of weighing the largest truck on the road, and free shower rooms for all truckers. The expansive parking lot provided room for truckers to park their rigs and get a few hours' worth of shuteye.

The old Flying A has been torn down, but another venerable establishment, Clark's Travel Center in Indio, Calif., was still in business as of 2020, offering "everything for the traveler, whether you are an RV'er, trucker, river rat or desert rat." Amenities included a truck wash, long-term parking, self-service laundry, 24-hour restaurant and car-truck wash.

Clark's, which opened in the 1940s, advertises itself as "the oldest operating truck stop on historic Route 99 from Canada to Mexico."

The restaurant at Klein's Truck Stop in the hamlet of Herndon, just north of Fresno, Calif., earned a reputation for serving some of the best breakfasts around. The restaurant stayed open into the new millennium before finally closing its doors, yielding to a Taco Bell and an am/pm minimart but leaving behind a huge parking lot as a place for truckers. One traveler from Los Angeles endorsed the now-closed coffee shop by stating that, no matter how hungry he might be, he always held his appetite in check if he were within 50 miles of Klein's.

Despite its popularity among the locals, there was no mistaking its target audience: the truck driver traveling the Main Street of California. When a truck driver came in, the hostess would usher him to the head of the line. The waitresses wore beehive hairdos, and each table had its own jukebox, offering up (of course) country music. The cooks made the kind of all-American fare that kept the belly feeling full for hours: hearty portions of chili, barbecue dishes, chicken-fried steak, their famous biscuits and gravy, and "pancakes as big and flat as Fresno."

Roy Cline opened Cline's Corners gas station and café in 1934 at the junction of New Mexico highways 6 and 2. At the time, Route 66 ran along a much longer path north through Santa Fe. In 1937, however, the federal government shortened the route by moving it to Highway 6 — but in the process, moved Highway 6 itself slightly to the north. This left Cline's place off the highway and forced him to move to stay in business.

Early on, Cline's Corners consisted of a small diner and two-pump Conoco station. It built a new building in the 1940s, with a tower promoting Gulf gasoline, then did another remodel and switched its fuel brand to Standard in the '50s as it continued to expand. At one point, it had a large "Travel Center" sign in the parking lot, but a cow (yes, a cow) crashed into it, having been lifted into the air and propelled by a wild windstorm.

Cline's added a small airport in the 1950s and a post office in 1964. Today, it includes a truck stop along with 30,000 square feet space that features a fast-food outlet, sit-down restaurant and large gift shop.

YESTERDAY'S HIGHWAYS

As time passed, places like Klein's were eclipsed by truck palaces called travel plazas or travel centers, giant complexes along 99, I-5 and other major highways that were affiliated with big chains.

The era of the interstate ushered in the trend toward travel centers, situated strategically at off-ramps, often between cities and towns along the way.

The first Pilot Truck Stop opened in 1958 in Gate City, Wash., two years after President Eisenhower signed the Interstate Act. Love's opened its first location in Watonga, Okla., in 1964.

And as the complexes grew bigger, a funny thing happened: Suddenly, they weren't just for truckers anymore. New convenience

A Flying J travel center off Interstate 5 near Lebec, Calif.

stores served as many travelers as truckers, selling touristy T-shirts and DVDs alongside motor oil and citizens band radio accessories.

Flying J, founded in 1968, recently offered such amenities as Subway and Denny's restaurants, 14 showers, a CAT scale, public laundry, video game arcade and ATMs at its site north of Bakersfield.

Other big chains followed: Truckstops of America, or TA, formed in 1972, and Petro launched in 1975. TA later changed its name to TravelCenters of America, reflecting its broader clientele, and bought out Petro in 2007. Three years later, Pilot acquired Flying J. In the new millennium, the number of truck stops (with at least one shower, diesel for sale and a minimum of 15 parking spaces) has grown to 2,500.

Trucks for sale along Interstate 10 in Southern California.

Roadside Stands to Restaurants

A Teen Burger from the A&W family stands atop a diner on California Route 41 south of Fresno.

Eat at Joe's

Drive down the interstate today, and you'll see the same thing over and over again. Golden arches rise at every third or fourth exit. If you're in the South, welcome to one Waffle House.

Then another.

Then another.

Starbucks. Dairy Queen. Subway. Cinnabon. Zaxby's. Cracker Barrel. The modern roadside is loaded with big chains that offer big portions of familiar products. You've been there before, a couple of hundred miles back, so you know what you're getting.

But there was a time when the American roadside was fertile ground for mom-and-pop coffee shops, diners and roadside stands in the shape of giant oranges, donuts and mugs of root beer.

Top: A sign from Paul's Donut Shop is preserved along U.S. 62 east of Evansville, Ind. **Above:** Today, this 18-foot-tall coffee pot stands alone along the Lincoln Highway in Bedford, Pa. But when it was built in 1927, it stood alongside a gas station. A decade later, a hotel was added, and the lunch spot was transformed into a bar.

The roadside eatery started small, before modern highways were born. In fact, early efforts had more in common with the neighborhood ice cream man, taco truck and your childhood lemonade stand than they did with KFC or Cracker Barrel.

Walter Scott didn't serve lemonade, but he did offer pies, boiled eggs, sandwiches and coffee to Rhode Island from a small, horse-drawn wagon he pulled up in front of the local newspaper.

YESTERDAY'S HIGHWAYS

The year was 1872. Sixteen years later, Thomas Buckley opened a nighttime food wagon called the Owl — the first of many such wagons he set up across the country. By the turn of the century, his Worcester Lunch Car Company opened some 275 of them, with names like White House Café and American Eagle Café.

Buckley's wagons weren't bare-bones. Equipped with stoves and iceboxes, they had barrel roofs and overhangs to keep customers from getting rained or snowed on while they ordered. Mahogany, silver and brass were among the materials he used. Colorful windows and lettering drew the eye, not unlike what you might see on a circus poster. Frosted glass on one model advertised "sandwiches, pies, milk and cigars" for sale. Sometimes, others bought the wagons and set up businesses of their own, but Buckley owned many himself and chose managers to run them.

He died in 1903 at just 35 years of age, but the trend he started continued to grow — as did the wagons themselves. With the autocar replacing the horse-drawn carriage as the preferred mode of transport, they became self-propelled. Smaller wheels replaced the spoked wagon wheels used for earlier models, and interiors were expanded to allow patrons to step inside.

Soon, some of the eateries jettisoned their wheels altogether and set up shop permanently at a single location. Many began to look less like wagons and more like the Pullman dining cars in use on passenger trains. Hence, the name "diner."

The shape is no accident. In fact, there's a practical reason for it. Like mobile homes, most diners were prefabricated and shipped from the factory to a given location. Since they had to be delivered by train or truck, they needed to fit on a long, narrow platform and, thus, wound up being shaped very much like the vehicles that carried them.

Over the years, some businessmen even bought converted rail or trolley cars and converted them into diners.

The Rock & Roll Diner on the Pacific Coast Highway in Oceano, Calif., is one example. When a new overpass on the highway left property owner Erl Sale with an oddly shaped, triangular plot of land, he hit on an idea. Sale, who had spent 13 years working as a Union Pacific dining car steward, decided to buy a couple of old rail cars from his former company and use them to serve "dinnah in a dinah," as he put it. The cars he purchased were an actual Pullman dining car from 1946 and a lounge car built the following year.

The Standard Diner in Fresno, Calif., opened in 1936 inside two former trolley cars from the Fresno Traction Company (dating from 1912 and 1925, respectively). It was still open years later, taking on the name Trolley Car Carole's in 1968, although it's closed today.

A pair of Los Angeles-area burger and hot dog diners called Carney's opened much later — one on Sunset Boulevard and the other in Studio City, along old U.S. 101 — aka Ventura Boulevard.

Above: Carney's "Express Limited" on Ventura Boulevard in Studio City, Calif., includes this dining car and red caboose mounted on a rail.

Right: A boarded-up Fresno Traction Company trolley was converted into the Standard Diner in Fresno, Calif.

Above: Railroad Park Resort in Dunsmuir, off old U.S. 99, offers a restaurant and motel rooms in converted rail cars.

A variation on the train-car idea: Aerodogs in Tulare, Calif., opened in 2006 using a 1951 Corvair T-29 training plane. It later became Richard's Lunchbox.

Because of their long, narrow shape, the dominant feature of most diners was an extended lunch counter lined with circular, usually backless, swivel stools. Like the downtown lunch counter, which it resembled, it was the ideal place for motorists to grab a quick cup of coffee, sandwich or slice of pie before hitting the road again.

Some diners also focused on grilled food, which helped earn them the nickname "greasy spoon." You might be able to order Adam and Eve on a Raft (two poached eggs on a piece of toast), a life preserver (donut), nervous pudding (Jell-O) or, of course, the ubiquitous blue-plate special. These were served, literally, on blue plates equipped with ridges to keep different foods in separate sections. They typically consisted of meat or fish in one section, potatoes in another, and veggies in a third.

The blue-plate special seems to have originated in the Harvey House restaurant chain, which sprang up along rail lines in the West before the age of the automobile. Owner Fred Harvey, who founded the company in 1876, wanted a way to serve train passengers quickly during brief station stops, and the blue-plate special was his solution. Harvey opened his first restaurant in Topeka, Kansas, along the Atchison, Topeka & Santa Fe line, and others followed. Unfortunately, when Route 66 opened and eclipsed the railcar as the preferred mode of overland transport, the Harvey Houses went into a slow decline.

Meanwhile, diners themselves began to change. The long, prefabricated buildings were joined along the roadside by new, larger structures built on site. Some mimicked the traditional diner style; others — Denney's, Sambo's, Bob's and others — retained the lunch counter within a more expansive layout. Many offered typical diner fare (coffee and sandwiches were always in demand), but some expanded their menus to include other items, as well.

The look of diners, prefab and otherwise, began to change in the 1930s, when the trend veered toward the then-new Art Deco and Streamline Moderne styles. One example: a chain of compact, boxy diners founded by Arthur Valentine along Route 66. Valentine produced the prefabricated buildings, which he sold to entrepreneurs who wanted a quick, simple way to get into restaurant business. They cost just $5,000, were easy to assemble, and were small enough — with just eight or ten stools (no booths or tables) — that they could be run by just a couple of people.

At their peak, Valentine Diners were operating in some 50 sites, many of them along Route 66.

YESTERDAY'S HIGHWAYS

Top: A Valentine Diner is preserved in the
parking lot of the Route 66 Museum in Clinton, Okla.
It opened in 1956 in Shamrock, Texas, and operated there until 1964.
Above: An abandoned diner built in a similar style sits by Route 66 in the ghost town of Glenrio, Texas. Once the Little Juarez Café, it has been vacant for years.

Taking a Stand

Diners had competition along the highway from roadside stands, forerunners of both the modern fast-food joint and the drive-in. One successful venture was the Giant Orange chain in California. The Giant Oranges were an early antidote to the stifling summer heat in Central California, where the thermometer can top out in the triple digits for days on end during July and August. Before the era of the air conditioner, one of the best ways to stay cool (and hydrated) was a cold drink, and what better candidate than orange juice? It helped that the fruit was plentiful in California, where the groves once blanketed much of the southern state.

Frank Pohl founded the first Giant Orange in 1926 along the Lincoln Highway in Tracy, Calif., serving juice out of a ten-foot-high stucco stand shaped like... a giant orange. He'd already tried a giant lemon, but it hadn't hit the spot. The orange, by contrast, proved so popular that other stands quickly followed, many of them along U.S Highway 99, which ran north and south through the heart of the state. They also spawned imitators with names like Mammoth Orange, Big Orange and Great Orange.

The oranges gradually disappeared as air conditioning became a common feature of most cars and highways were upgraded to eliminate stoplights and replace intersections with off-ramps. *The Long Beach Independent* reported that the last one, in Dixon, Calif., closed in 1973, with a story headlined "Freeway squeezes Giant Orange dry." (For more on the Giant Oranges, see my book *Highway 99: The History of California's Main Street*).

An inside view of an old Mammoth Orange stand, sitting in a field in Chowchilla, Calif. The stands once served motorists on U.S. 99 and other California highways in places like Redding, Placerville, Galt, Madera and Bakersfield.

YESTERDAY'S HIGHWAYS

Orange juice wasn't the only kind of refreshment offered along the highway. Root beer was a hit, too. Roy Allen opened a roadside stand in Lodi, Calif., in 1919 and later added partner Frank Wright, creating the name A&W from their initials. The company's second restaurant, in Sacramento, was considered the first drive-in, with "tray boys" providing curbside service.

On hot days, naturally, root beer floats — featuring vanilla ice cream — proved especially popular. That idea was still relatively new: In 1893, a Colorado brewer noticed that the snow on nearby Cow Mountain looked like ice cream floating in soda. So he decided to try combining the two ingredients, calling his invention a Black Cow.

In the early days, roadside stands tended to focus on one specialty item, whether it be orange juice, root beer, fried chicken, donuts or hot dogs. Only later did they add other menu items, most commonly burgers and fries. (The Mammoth Orange in Fairmead, Calif., promised "Alaska-sized" burgers, in contrast to a competitor's "Texas-sized" offering.) But the signature item on the menu remained the main draw. Nowhere was this obvious than behind the counter of the ice cream parlor.

These businesses were popular in city centers, where they were often known as soda fountains, but were also plentiful on the highway. Even today, you see a lot of ice cream spots beside the road. It's no mystery why: Ice cream cools you down even better than orange juice or root beer, and the "are we there yet?" kids love it. Chains like Dairy Queen, Fosters Freeze, Tastee-Freez and, in Central California, Sno-White Drive In began appearing on roadsides in the 1940s, with many other independent stands and stops filling the gaps in between.

Dairy Queen was founded in 1940 along State Route 53 in Joliet, Ill., using a soft-serve substance that swirls from a dispenser rather than being scooped from a tub. The cool treat would become popular in years to come. A former DQ employee started Tastee-Freez, also in Joliet, in 1950.

Out West, Fosters Freeze got its start on La Brea Avenue in La Brea, Calif., in 1946; Sno-White began in Stockton, Calif., during the 1950s and boasted 200 locations at the height of its popularity — all in the Golden State between Chico and Bakersfield, except for two in Guam.

Another soft-serve company, Dari-Delite, grew to 300 independently franchised stores in 32 states (including 50 in California) by 1962. And then there were Twistee Treets, which started in Florida during early 1980s. The company produced about 90 of its distinctive buildings, shaped like soft-serve cones with a cherry on top. Twistee Treets went out of business, but some of the buildings are still in business under other names, including one on the Lincoln Highway in Massillon, Ohio (below), and another in St. Joseph, Mo. (bottom).

YESTERDAY'S HIGHWAYS

A&W started a promotional campaign in 1963 that featured the "Burger Family" — fiberglass statues that represented different menu items dubbed Papa, Mama and Baby Burger (a Teen Burger was added the following year).

Right: The Papa Burger statue, minus the A&W logo, remains at Angelo's Burgers off U.S. 101 in Oceanside, Calif.

Below: The family, seen here off Route 66 at Rollo, Mo., gave way in 1974 to the "Great Root Bear" ad campaign.

From top: Dairy delights along yesterday's highways came in all shapes and sizes. An ice cream shop on a highway near Berlin, Conn., came in the shape of boxed containers. It also served "milk drinks," along with toasted sandwiches, "frankfurts" and "hamburgs" when Lee Russell snapped this photo in 1939. An Albuquerque café on Route 66 was shaped like a pair of icebergs in Russell's 1940 shot. The Milk Bottle Dairy Bar & Restaurant on Route 138 in Taunton, Mass. *Library of Congress photos*

YESTERDAY'S HIGHWAYS

From top: A Dairy Queen sign in on Route 66 in Holbrook, Ariz.; Foster's Freeze off U.S. 101 in San Luis Obispo, Calif., closed recently; Tastee-Freez on U.S. 29 in Madison, Va.

From top: Jolly Kone on California Highway 46 in Wasco; an ice cream stand on Route 66 in Joliet, Ill., where both Dairy Queen and Tastee-Freez were born; a Frostie sign on old U.S. 101 in Ukiah, Calif.

YESTERDAY'S HIGHWAYS

Clockwise from top: Dairy King in southwestern Missouri (U.S. 66), Dairy Barn in St. Joseph, Kan. (U.S. 36), and Colleen's Drive-In in Arrington, Va. (US 29).

Coffee Shops to Carhops

One ice cream stand built on its early success to develop a roadside empire. Howard Johnson developed a menu of 28 ice cream flavors and, in 1925, he began selling them alongside hot dogs and soda on a beach in Massachusetts. Within a few years, Johnson had obtained a loan to open a full-fledged restaurant in Quincy, Mass., that also featured such items as baked beans, chicken pot pies and fried clams.

Over the middle part of the 20th century, Johnson's restaurants became roadside staples. Here's how it happened: After a period of growth — through some of the first franchise agreements — in the late 1930s, the chain nearly disappeared during World War II. But then, Johnson earned a major coup: As the nation began to build new roads, he won exclusive rights to position his restaurants at turnoffs on the Ohio, Pennsylvania, New Jersey and Connecticut turnpikes. Just as Richfield had done with its Beacon tower stations, Johnson set out to plant restaurants every 50 miles or so along the highway.

Travelers could be sure they'd see the same menu at each location, so they knew what they were getting. All they had to do was look for the next orange roof with its blue cupola or spire, topped by a weathervane. The colonial-style buildings were instantly recognizable.

Margie's Diner off U.S. 101 in San Luis Obispo is a former Howard Johnson's. The base for the old spire/weathervane is still visible on the roof, which retains flecks of its original orange paint.

YESTERDAY'S HIGHWAYS

Left: Howard Johnson's began adding motels with distinctive gabled roofs — such as this one off U.S. 101 in San Luis Obispo, Calif. — in 1954.

Above: A Howard Johnson's postcard touts its 28 flavors of ice cream, fried clams, daily lunch specials and special "frankforts," together with steaks, chops, chicken and lobsters.

Howard Johnson added its first motel in 1954, in Savannah, Ga., and the chain grew to more than 1,000 restaurants and 500 motor lodges by the late 1970s, when it was the nation's largest restaurant chain.

Howard Johnson's success paved the way for scores of similar coffeeshops, diners and casual restaurants that came to dominate the roadside in the second half of the century.

While HoJo got its start with ice cream, Georgia-based Stuckey's originated as a lean-to shed where W.S. Stuckey sold pecans in 1934. He built his first full-fledged store three years later, featuring his wife's homemade pecan log roles and divinity, then added a restaurant along with a novelty store and gas pumps.

As the chain grew, Stuckey tried to branch out into roadside inns, as Howard Johnson had done, but only managed to build four of them before selling his business to Pet, Inc. The restaurant/store combos, however, continued to prosper, and the chain reached a peak of more than 350 locations in the 1960s. It also gave birth, in a roundabout way, to another prominent roadside chain, called Horne's.

Bob Horne was actually an employee of Stuckey's before he struck out on his own. Horne apparently made candy for Stuckey's, but parted ways with his employer over a dispute of some sort. He then opened what became a chain of restaurants across the Southeast in steeply sloped A-frame buildings with bright yellow roofs that resembled the early Stuckey's design.

Horne also followed Stuckey's example of selling novelty items and gas as part of his business, opening a full-fledged gift shop. In the restaurant, he created a "Circus Grille" with clown-themed decor to appeal to the kids. Bright red, blue, orange and pink stripes accented a canopy over a horseshoe-shaped lunch counter (booth seating was also available). Breakfast was typical diner fare: In 1970, you could get hot cakes with sausage or bacon for $1.25, cinnamon toast for 50 cents or two scrambled eggs with sugar-cured ham and hash browns for $1.50.

Bob Horne sold his business to Greyhound, which had already set up Post House restaurants in its terminals to serve bus travelers, and the chain went national. Soon, Horne's locations sprang up as far north as Michigan and as far west as California, with locations along major highways such as U.S. 99 in Central California and Route 66 in Chenoa, Ill., north of Bloomington.

At its peak, Greyhound was serving 275 million meals a year at Horne's and Post House. Overnight accommodations were added, following the Howard Johnson's model and patterned after Holiday Inn. Greyhound even floated a fast-food concept called Hornette in 1967. But two years later, the bus company sold Horne's to a company called

YESTERDAY'S HIGHWAYS

Stand 'N' Snack. At that point, Horne's had 19 motor lodges to go with 72 restaurants, but things began to go downhill from there. Locations began to close, and there were only 16 restaurants still in business. For many years, an abandoned Horne's building could be seen along Highway 99 in the San Joaquin Valley hamlet of Traver.

Today, one location remains: in Port Royal, Va.

Top: A car whizzes past a billboard for Stuckey's on Interstate 95 in this photo by Thomas J. O'Halloran from 1965. *Library of Congress*. **Above:** A postcard for Horne's Motor Lodge and Restaurant, with the chain's distinctive A-frame roof and crown logo atop the sign.

Greyhound's ownership of the Post House and Horne's restaurant chains, was, of course, a sideline to its main business: interstate bus service. Carl Wickman started Greyhound in 1913 after his Hupmobile car franchise failed. For his first route, a mere two miles between Hibbing and Alice, Minn., he charged 15 iron miners 15 cents each for a ride in his eight-seat "touring car." It was the beginning of intercity bus travel.

The company got its name in the 1920s, when one of its drivers saw his bus reflected in a store window, and it reminded him of a greyhound. By 2013, the company had 2,000 buses serving 3,800 destinations in 48 states and nine Canadian provinces. *Above: a Greyhound depot in Fresno.*

YESTERDAY'S HIGHWAYS

Other restaurant chains snapped up prime highway real estate, as well. Among them were Bob Evans, which was founded in 1948 and had 500 Midwestern and Mid-Atlantic locations as of 2020. Even more successful was Cracker Barrel, a country-style restaurant with a big gift shop, that started in 1969 in Lebanon, Tenn. By 2019, it had 660 restaurants in 45 states.

Both Bob Evans and Cracker Barrel offered all-day breakfast service, but one chain went even further, staying open all night and tying its identity to a single breakfast dish: the waffle.

Waffle House, founded in 1955, by a former cook for another all-night roadside stop called Toddle House. As of 2015, it had grown to 2,100 location, ten times the size of Toddle House at its peak. A weird combination of a fast-food restaurant and a greasy-spoon diner, it's described in the 1996 movie *Tin Cup* as a "low-rent roadside café featuring waffles." But Waffle House is nothing if not durable. It's become famous for remaining open, no matter what — so much so that Craig Fugate, the Federal Emergency Management Agency's chief, took notice. In 2011, two Waffle House restaurants in Joplin, Mo., remained open amid a massive tornado that killed 158 people and became the costliest twister in U.S. history.

Fugate later remarked, "If you get there (to a disaster site) and the Waffle House is closed? That's really bad." The agency created what it called the Waffle House Index to measure the severity of storms by color. On the green level, the restaurant is open and largely undamaged; at yellow, the power is out; at the red level, the place is closed.

Rivaling the success of Waffle House is Denny's, which started out like many others focusing on a single menu item. But you might not be able to guess what it was, because it's not something the chain is known for today.

Denny's started out in the Los Angeles area as *Danny's* Donuts — even though neither of its founders was named Danny (or Denny, for that matter). The chain founded by Harold Butler and Richard Jezak in 1953 switched from donuts to a coffeeshop motif three years later, and it wasn't until 1959 that it changed its name to Denny's. The motive was pure marketing: a desire to avoid confusion with a local competitor called Coffee Dan's. In many ways, Denny's became the successor to Howard Johnson's, which saw its star fade at the end of the 20th century, with only a single restaurant remained (in Lake George, N.Y.) by 2018. But Denny's continued to thrive.

The chain now has some 1,700 locations. It introduced its signature item, the Grand Slam Breakfast, in 1977 to celebrate the retirement of Hank Aaron, then baseball's all-time home run leader. Twenty years later, it added a second format, Denny's Diner, a more streamlined concept that harkened back to the roots of roadside restaurants.

In fact, most coffeehouses in the second half of the 20th century were built around the diner concept. They simply added tables and booths to larger, permanent structures built around the traditional long counter with stools. Howard Johnson's did it. So did Denny's and countless others, like Bob's and Sambo's. (Some added backs to the old round swivel stools to make patrons feel a bit more comfortable — and a bit less rushed.)

Bob's on Riverside Drive in Burbank, Calif., opened in 1949 and still operates, just a short distance off U.S. 101. It combined drive-in service with an interior coffeeshop.

One of the most successful of these was Big Boy, which actually preceded Denny's by nearly two decades. Founded in 1936 as Bob's Pantry, it was one of the first restaurants built around a burger: the Big Boy was the first double-decker hamburger, and it gave the chain its name.

Howard Johnson's had a recognizable logo featuring Simple Simon and the Pieman, characters from an 18th century English nursery rhyme. But Bob's logo proved even more memorable: a big-eyed, big-bellied boy with wavy hair and checkerboard suspenders, holding a hamburger on a tray.

Founder Bob Wian offered curbside drive-in service and expanded eastward by licensing his Big Boy hamburger to restaurateurs like Frisch's in Cincinnati, Eat'n Park in Pittsburgh, and Shoney's in Charleston, W.V. Shoney's, named for founder Alex Schoenbaum, became the largest purveyor of Big Boy burgers, with 392 outlets by 1984. It was in that Orwellian year, however, that the chain withdrew from the franchise and stopped serving the iconic burger.

Still, the memory of that connection remained a decade later, when country singer Joe Diffie released a song called *Third Rock from the Sun*. The tune included a line in which a car hits a Big Boy statue in a Shoney's parking lot, causing a power outage.

Another major coffeehouse chain, Sambo's, looked similar to Denny's inside and out: Even the shape of the sign wasn't all that different.

Sambo's, founded in 1957, took its name from letters in the two founders' names: *Sam* Battistone and Newell *Boh*nett. It built its menu around pancakes and its image around an 1899 children's story of an East Indian boy and his tussle with some tigers who want to steal his clothes. The story of *Little Black Sambo* must have seemed like a perfect fit, considering the restaurant's name — not to mention how the tale ends: The tigers all become jealous and start to chase one another in circles, running so fast they turn into butter. Sambo's father finds the butter and brings it home, and his mother uses it to make…

Pancakes.

The problem with the story was that Sambo had often been depicted, in various copies of the books, not as a turbaned Indian boy (as he was in story panels at the restaurant), but as an extremely racist caricature of an *African* child. The prominence of the boy's color in the title of the book didn't help, nor did the fact that the Spanish word "zambo" was used in referring to children of Africans and Native Americans.

The controversy led the restaurant to rebrand locations with various names such as Seasons, the Jolly Tiger, and No Place Like Sam's. But the controversy, along with a profit-sharing plan that ran off the rails, sent the chain into a tailspin. At the end of the 1970s, it had more than 1,100 locations; today, it's down to just one, in Santa Barbara, Calif.

An IHOP restaurant on San Fernando Boulevard in Burbank, Calif., complete with the chain's early and iconic A-frame roof, reminiscent in some ways of the Howard Johnson's look.

Another pancake-centric chain has proven more durable. IHOP was born just a year after Sambo's as International House of Pancakes. Like Denny's, Sambo's and Bob's, the pancake house has its roots in Southern California. But its A-frame design owed something to Howard Johnson's: Its roof tiles were blue instead of orange, but the buildings also featured orange accents. External wooden beams, as in the Tudor style, and faux gas lamps on the top of signage added to their European flavor.

Menus in the 1960s featured items with a geographic flair, such as Maine Blueberry Pancakes, Viennese Potato Pancakes, Brazilian Banana Pancakes and Tropical Tahitian

Pancakes, as well as a section titled *Hamburgers from Around the World.*

But "International House of Pancakes" was quite a mouthful, so the chain shortened its name to IHOP and adopted a kangaroo mascot in the early 1970s. Since then, the chain has largely forsaken its iconic look in favor of more generic, boxy structures, with the last A-frame model going up in 1979.

It had more than 1,800 locations as of 2019, including some in the Middle East.

Pea Soup Andersen's original location on U.S. 101 in Buellton, **top**, and a later addition to the chain in Selma on Highway 99, **right**, which subsequently closed and became a steakhouse — though it still served pea soup.

As time passed, some roadside coffeeshops grew even larger, becoming destinations in their own right. Pea Soup Andersen's in California was one example. Although it never had a large number of locations, the locations it did operate were large. They came complete with extensive gift and sweet shops to rival those at Cracker Barrel.

Whereas some restaurants built themselves around donuts or burgers, Andersen's offered a more unusual signature item: pea soup. The business' mascots, a rotund chef named Hap-Pea and his petrified pea-splitting partner, Pee-Wee, bore a passing resemblance to Simon and the Pieman on Howard Johnson's iconic logo, but were more fun and endearing.

The business was founded in 1924 in Buellton, Calif., along what would become U.S. Highway 101. Andersen's expanded to a second location in 1976, at the Interstate 5 offramp stop of Santa Nella to the north, later adding restaurants in Carlsbad, Mammoth Lakes and Selma, Calif. All except the Santa Nella restaurant later closed, although the Selma location morphed into a restaurant called the Spike 'n' Rail — which still served pea soup.

Andersen's is known for its giant windmills, easily visible from the highway. (For more on the chain, see my book *Highway 101: The History of El Camino Real*.)

Roadside restaurants on U.S. 101 in the Salinas Valley, **above**, and on Route 66 in Santa Rosa, N.M., **left**.

YESTERDAY'S HIGHWAYS

From top: Farnesi's, a longtime fixture on Highway 99 in the Madera area of California; Norm's on State Route 39 (Beach Boulevard) in Huntington Beach; and the Hollywood Café on old 99 in Lodi.

Mr. D'z Route 66 Diner is a nostalgic trip back to the 1950s filled with memorabilia amid pastel pink and turquoise colors, with a checkerboard floor and a long diner with swivel stools. There's also a vintage patrol car out front. The eatery in Kingman, Ariz., opened in 1939 as the Kingman Café and Kimo Shell Station. It was remodeled in the 1980s.

YESTERDAY'S HIGHWAYS

Tommy's along old U.S. 101 in San Clemente was once a favorite stop for Richard Nixon.

While some restaurants grew bigger, others grew faster. As the car culture boomed in the postwar years, restaurateurs sought ways to cater to motorists looking for a quick bite. Diners with swivel stools were fine for a cup of coffee, but you still had to get out of your car. Drive-ins with carhops and jukeboxes became popular in the 1950s, giving drivers an alternative to a sit-down meal — and offering teens a place to congregate on Friday nights.

The first drive-in predated the fabulous fifties, though. Kirby's Pig Stand pioneered the concept when it opened the first such eatery in 1921 on the highway between Dallas and Fort Worth, Texas.

"People with cars are so lazy they don't want to get out of them to eat!" founder J.G. Kirby mused.

The concept, built around a barbecue pork sandwich, was an immediate hit, with motorists from all over converging on the small corner lot and placing their orders with carhops. These young men were snappy dressers, attired in white shirts and hats with bowties. (They must have needed to be careful not to get barbecue sauce on their uniforms.) Why the name "carhops"? The eager servers had the habit of running up to approaching customers and hopping on the running boards before they'd even stopped.

The Pig Stand was so popular it soon became a chain, offering "Quick Curb Service" and dishing up "America's Motor Lunch." Four years after the first stand opened, there were six of them in Dallas, and the chain quickly expanded beyond its point of origin. The Kirby family operated most of the Texas locations, while franchisees opened Pig Stands in Alabama, Arkansas, California, Florida, Louisiana, Mississippi, New York and Oklahoma. More than 120 stands were opened between 1921 and 1934.

By the mid-'20s, most new Pig Stands were wood-framed buildings covered in stucco and topped by a red roof reminiscent of a pagoda. A 1927 newspaper ad claimed more than 5,000 in Dallas ate their dinners at a Pig Stand. Four years later, a grab-and-go service window for bagged meals was added at a Los Angeles location.

In 1998, *Houston Chronicle* reviewer Ken Hoffman proclaimed that "the Pig Stand is to fast food what Cooperstown is to baseball: It's where it all started."

The Pig Stand didn't just invent the drive-in and drive-through ideas, it was the first to serve fried onion rings, a chicken-fried steak sandwich and Texas toast. The onion rings were really an accident: Someone dropped some raw onion slices into a bowl of batter meant for chicken-fried steak.

Other drive-ins eventually caught up with the Pig Stand, and all except the Texas locations had closed by the end of the fifties. But by that time, it had spawned a host of other eateries seeking to cash in on the pork sandwich craze. Frith's Dixie Pig Bar-B-Q, opened in 1954 off U.S. 220 in southern Virginia. It was still family-operated in 2019, operating today in a 1985 brick building with plenty of inside seating. But the neon sign out front (seen above) still advertises "curb service," and a photo of the original building inside the restaurant shows a rectangular building not unlike photos of early Pig Stands.

Drive-in restaurants competed with one another to see which ones could provide the fastest service. Some put carhops on roller skates. Others installed speaker systems with names like Auto-O-Hop, Fon-A-Chef and Dine-a-Mike.

YESTERDAY'S HIGHWAYS

Clockwise from top left: The former Jan's Dutch Boy Drive-In on U.S. 220 in Collinsville, Va., now operates as Taqueria La Juquilita; the sign is all that remains of the old Windmill Drive-In near Selma on Highway 99 in California; a sign for a "Drive-Inn" described as the "Home of Quality Food on Route 66 in Tucumcari, N.M.

Top: Bill's Take Out was built in 1953 on Broadway (old U.S. 101) in Santa Maria.
Above: Pick's Drive In of Cloverdale, Calif., dates all the way back to 1923 on 101.

Top: The Little Chef Diner was built in 1952 in Danville, Va., and moved to its current spot on Main Street (State Route 293) in the 1960s. It's a Valentine diner.

Right: The Ludlow Café in California's Mojave Desert on Route 66 is the second establishment to bear that name, having replaced a now demolished boxy building that stood nearby dated back at least to the 1940s.

From top: The Ku-Ku on Route 66 in Miami, Okla., is a remnant of a chain that once included more than 200 outlets in the Midwest; Fat Daddy's Chill Grill on the Ohio River Scenic Byway in Grandview, Ohio; the menu at Ridgeway Drive-In off U.S. 220 in southern Virginia.

YESTERDAY'S HIGHWAYS

Right: A McDonald's sign on California Route 126 in Fillmore features the chain's early mascot, a cartoon chef named Speedee. **Below:** A 1955 McDonald's in Fresno has been remodeled to recapture its original look.

Another restaurant that just might have been inspired by the Pig Stand is the one that would go on to become the undisputed king of fast food: McDonald's.

When Dick and Mac McDonald opened their first restaurant at 14th and E streets in San Bernardino way back in 1940, they employed carhops and offered a menu that featured pork sandwiches and barbecued ribs. It wasn't until eight years later that they changed their format to focus on burgers, shakes and sodas, firing their carhops and setting the stage for the modern fast-food craze.

In doing so, they were following in the footsteps of another early fast-food pioneer: White Castle, which traced its origins to a Wichita streetcar diner way back in 1916. Walter Anderson transformed the hamburger from a novelty item sold on boardwalks and at county fairs into a fast-food staple. Anderson had expanded to three diners by 1921, when he took on a partner named Billy Ingram, with whom he developed a new branding concept: white restaurants (to denote cleanliness) shaped like castles (for stability). Hence the name, White Castle.

Left: Early burger joints were little more than roadside stands, like this makeshift diner in Harlingen, Texas, photographed by Lee Russell in 1939. *Library of Congress*

Above, left: White Castle spawned imitators like White Crystal in Monmoth, N.J. and White Tower in Amsterdam, N.Y. *Library of Congress*

YESTERDAY'S HIGHWAYS

Like Wendy's decades later, White Castle served burgers with square patties — but they were a lot smaller: about 2 inches across. White Castle called them "sliders," either because they slid across the griddle, slid easily out of their boxes, or slid down smoothly as you ate them. They were later trademarked as "Slyders" by the chain.

White Castle's first five restaurants were in Wichita, but it expanded to Omaha in 1921 and to other Midwestern cities — Chicago, Cincinnati, Columbus, Detroit, Kansas City, Louisville, Minneapolis, St. Louis — in the mid-1920s. It reached the East Coast in 1930, when eateries appeared in New York and Newark, and a year later, it had 115 locations.

White Castle's tiny burgers were perfect for quick consumption. And low prices. In the early '60s, the chain was offering five hamburgers for 24 cents re-entered. The chain endures today and re-entered popular culture in 2004, thanks to a stoner comedy called *Harold & Kumar Go to White Castle*. The chain was never franchised and remains family owned, with nearly 400 locations in the Midwest and East.

Over the years, the White Castle System (its formal name) spawned a variety of imitators, many of them using variations of the White Castle name. Among the first was White Tower, founded in 1926 in Milwaukee, which grew to 230 locations by the mid-1950s. White Hut was founded in 1935 in Toledo, and Royal Castle got off the ground in 1938 in Miami.

Another Midwest imitator, Hill's Snappy Service, offered 5-cent burgers and, like White Castle, invited customers to "buy 'em by the sack." The chain was a big success in the 1930s and early '40s, but its reliance on walk-in customers proved its undoing when Americans took to the road after World War II. Still, Snappy Service helped set the stage for McDonald's new approach when the brothers ditched their original barbecue drive-in format and turned to burgers.

They adapted the assembly line to the food industry and set up what they called their "Speedee Service System," adopting as their mascot a cartoon chef named Speedee (with a hamburger head) who predated Ronald McDonald. In 1955, the chain opened its second franchise location, on State Highway 41 in Fresno, at the corner of Blackstone and Shields Avenues. The first franchise, in Illinois, belonged to a mixer salesman named Ray Kroc who saw the restaurants as a way to market his mixers.

The Fresno franchise holder, Art Bender, eventually owned seven McDonald's and

Kroc wound up buying the chain outright from Mac McDonald in 1961 for a cool $2.7 million.

That year, the chain's ads were still calling it a drive-in — "The Drive-in with the Arches."

"McDonald's Amazing Menu" offered any of the following for just a dime:

- Golden French Fries
- Thirst-Quenching Coke
- Delightful Root Beer
- Steaming Hot Coffee
- Full-Flavor Orange Drink
- Refreshing Cold Milk

You could grab a "Pure Beef Hamburger" for 15 cents, a "Tempting Cheeseburger" for 19 cents or a "Triple Thick Shake" for 20 cents — the most expensive item on the menu. The 15-cent price was the standard for fast-food burgers in the late 1950s and early '60s.

Hardee's sold 15-cent burgers, too. So did Virginia-based Kenney's (which sold "thick milk shakes" for a dime, half of what McDonald's was charging for its "triple thick" shakes). And Burger Chef, one of McDonald's biggest competitors, was still selling "nickel and dime" hamburgers in 1967. In fact, Burger Chef ranked as the No. 2 fast-food chain with 1,200 locations in 1972, second only to McDonald's 1,600.

Burger Chef got started in 1958. Its name was reportedly chosen to reflect a more upscale alternative to Burger King, which had opened five years earlier, and it was the first chain to offer the now-ubiquitous basic combo of burger, fries and a drink. (The so-called "Triple Threat" sold for 45 cents.) Its owners also patented the flame broiler and set up a system that could produce 800 burgers per hour — more than even McDonald's could manage.

Burger Chef was a trailblazer in healthy food, too: In 1973, it added a salad bar, becoming one of the earliest fast-food places to do so.

It also beat McDonald's to the punch in appealing to kids. Many people remember Ronald McDonald and his friends from the 1970s ad campaign: the Hamburglar, Mayor McCheese, Captain Crook and a purple monster named the Grimace, to name a few. But fewer recall that Burger Chef had a similar group of characters geared toward the younger set. There were two mascots: Burger Chef and his young sidekick, Jeff, along with a vampire called Count Fangburger, a witch named Cackleburger, a magician called Burgerini and a talking ape named Burgerilla.

Burger Chef tied these characters to something called a Funmeal, which included toys and puzzles for the kids. If this sounds a lot like McDonald's Happy Meal... well, Burger Chef thought so, too. When McDonald's came out with its version six years *after* the Funmeal made its debut, Burger Chef sued.

And lost.

By the late 1960s, the chain had expanded into as many 39 states; but despite its innovations during the following decade, it soon went into a tailspin. Even the marketing coup of a lifetime couldn't save Burger Chef: It signed a licensing deal in 1978 with *Star Wars* for seven themed Funmeals. One of the cardboard boxes could be punched out to create the pieces of C-3PO, which could be assembled to create a "droid puppet." (Other boxes let you punch out figures of R2-D2, a land speeder, X-wing fighter and TIE fighter; one contained a Darth Vader card game.) The chain also gave away a free *Star Wars* movie poster to any customer who ordered a large Coke, and the campaign even saw R2-D2 and C-3PO appear in a Burger Chef commercial.

None of this was enough to save the Chef. General Foods, which owned the chain, sold it to Hardee's parent company in 1982, and many of the stores were converted to the Hardee's nameplate. The last restaurant under the Burger Chef name closed in 1996.

Chains like Burger King, Wendy's and Jack-in-the-Box tried to challenge McDonald's for preeminence in the burger market over the next several years, with several other burger joints popping up, as well. Among them:

- Biff Burger
- Carl's Jr. (which later merged with Hardee's)
- In-N-Out
- Rally's
- Whataburger
- Fatburger
- Sonic

Sonic was, in fact, one of the few — and by far the most successful — chains to retain its drive-in identity. Founded in 1953 in Oklahoma as Top Hat Drive-In, it changed its name in 1959 to emphasize its "service with the speed of sound" motto. (Besides, "Top Hat" was already trademarked.) As of 2020, it had a total of more than 3,500 locations.

An abandoned Sonic restaurant on U.S. Business 58 in Martinsville, Va.

The early Pig Stand craze notwithstanding, burgers have remained the most popular signature item at fast-food eateries for decades. It's not even really close. Chicken ranked second in the early 1970s before pizza pulled ahead. Mexican checks in at No. 4.

In many cases, one or two chains emerged to dominate the market in each of several specialties:

Sub Sandwiches

Subway, founded in 1965 as Pete's Super Submarines, had more sub-sandwich restaurants than any of its competitors as of 2019. Its 41,500 eateries far outpaced hoagie rivals like Blimpie, Jersey Mike's, Jimmy John's, Togo's, Quiznos and Submarina. In fact, it had more locations worldwide than any other restaurant, period. Yes, that includes McDonald's and Starbucks.

Mexican

Taco Bell, named for founder Glen Bell, started out as a hot dog stand in San Bernardino in 1962. Yes, that's the same place McDonald's started. As of 2018, none of its major competitors — Chipotle, Qboda, Moe's or Del Taco — had even half its 7,000 locations. Taco Bell's early menu featured five items for a quarter each: taco, tostada, burritos with red or green sauce, frijoles (beans with cheese on top) and the Bellburger. This last item was later renamed the Bell Beefer and ultimately dropped from the menu altogether.

A seafood stop called the Clam Box could be found along Route 1-A in Ipswitch, Mass. *Library of Congress*

Seafood

Long John Silver's outlasted rivals like Arthur Treacher's and Skipper's. Both Long John Silver's and Arthur Treacher's were founded in 1969 — the former in Kentucky and the latter in Columbus, Ohio. Arthur Treacher's was named after an English character actor known for playing butlers who later served as Merv Griffin's talk-show sidekick. Arthur Treacher, the actor, served as a spokesman for Arthur Treacher's, the restaurant. It was the top fish-and-chips stop in the late 1970s, when it had about 800 sites; but it was down to just seven by 2019; at that point LJS had more than 1,000.

Sanders Court in Corbin, Ky., is pictured on this vintage postcard.

Chicken

In 1930, Harland Sanders started selling his fried chicken at a Shell station on U.S. Route 25 outside North Corbin, Ky. The 40-year-old Sanders had already worked and a railroad man and a tire salesman. He'd made some money running a ferry boat company, then lost it investing in acetylene lamps. Sanders bought an Asheville, N.C., motel in 1939 and built a restaurant alongside it; he franchised his secret recipe in 1952. As of 2019, the chain that grew out of Sanders' "original recipe" of 11 herbs and spices had more than 22,000 locations worldwide, outpacing the likes of Chick-fil-A, Popeye's, Zaxby's and Bojangles'. An early competitor, take-out king Chicken Delight, was founded in 1952 and grew to more than 1,000 locations in the 1960s powered by its jingle, "Don't cook tonight. Call Chicken Delight!" It had just 26 locations left as of 2019.

Pizza

As of 2019, Domino's and Pizza Hut were battling for the top spot among fast-food pizza chains, with Little Caesar's running third. Pizza Hut was founded in 1958 in Wichita, Kan., and had more than 18,000 locations as of 2019, about 2,000 more than Domino's, which opened its first store two years later in Ypsilanti, Mich. Pizza Hut, like KFC and Taco Bell, is owned by Yum! Brands (which also owned Long John Silver's and A&W until 2011).

Donuts

Dunkin' Donuts, founded in 1950 in Massachusetts, had nearly 13,000 sites as of 2019, far ahead of Krispy Kreme (about 1,000), which dates back to 1937 in Winston-Salem, N.C. Winchell's Donut House, founded in 1948, was a big player in California for many years, with 870 locations in the West and Midwest by 1982. Once owned by Denney's, it was purchased by Yum-Yum donuts in 2004 and was down to 170 stores in six states by 2020.

Hot Dogs

Wienerschnitzel touts itself as the World's Largest Hot Dog Chain. Founded in 1961 by a former Taco Bell employee named John Galardi, it was originally known as Der Wienerschnitzel. The name was a bit odd: In German, *wiener shnitzel* doesn't refer to hot dogs, but to Vienna-style veal. To make matters worse, the proper article would have been *das*, not *der*. The company dropped the article altogether in 1977. Der Wienerschnitzels were in A-frame buildings, similar to (but smaller than) early IHOPs. Some even had drive-thru lanes that went directly *through* the building. Wienerschnitzel had 358 locations as of 2020. Other hot dog chains over the years have included Dog n Suds, an Illinois-based chain started in 1953 that also featured root beer and grew to 680 locations 15 years later (17 remain today). Pup 'N' Taco, which opened in Pasadena in 1956, served an odd combination of hot dogs, tacos and pastrami sandwiches. It had grown to 104 locations by 1984, at which point most were sold to Taco Bell.

Roast Beef

Arby's, the chain with the big cowboy hat, was founded in 1964 in Ohio and went on to become the nation's biggest roast beef sandwich shop with nearly 3,500 locations as of 2019. It was also the second-biggest sandwich chain overall, after Subway. The chain was founded by Leroy and Forrest Raffel, the Raffel Brothers — or R.B. Hence, the restaurant's name. (No, it doesn't stand for roast beef.)

A sign for Ben's Café on U.S. 6 in Green River, Utah.

Inns and Motels

The Blue Swallow Motel opened on Route 66 in Tucumcari, N.M., with ten rooms and is still operating today. Two more units were added in 1948, creating the current configuration.

Room at the Inn

It would be easy to think motels developed out of hotels. Even the name "motel" is a mashup of the words "motor" and "hotel." But motels didn't start out as second-rate hotels by the side of the road. They weren't a different kind of hotel, but *an alternative to* hotels.

If roadside restaurants started out as food wagons, motels began as campgrounds — or something close.

Each of the two world wars was followed by a period of prosperity when Americans took to the open road. They had more freedom, more money and more time to explore. They also had a fast-improving road system that took them farther and moved them faster than ever before.

The period after World War II is fresher in our memories. We've heard about how Americans released years of pent-up frustration at the rationing of gas, tires and cars themselves. For four years, automobile factories had been engaged in making tanks, planes and other wartime necessities. But with the end of the war, those factories started making up for lost time by cranking out cars faster than ever before, while newly prosperous — and optimistic — Americans were buying them. Meanwhile, the government was building new highways at an unprecedented rate, in anticipation of the interstate initiative ten years later.

What's often forgotten is that something very similar happened after World War I. Before the U.S. entered the war, President Woodrow Wilson had signed a bill dedicating $75 million for road improvements, but by 1919, only $500,000 of that total had been spent and just 12 miles of road had been built.

Eisenhower served as an interesting link between the two eras: In 1919, as a lieutenant colonel in the U.S. Army, he took part in a cross-country convoy of 72 military vehicles along the Lincoln Highway, and saw firsthand just how bad even the nation's most celebrated roads were. Some days, they managed to cover no more than 3 miles. The vehicles broke down, got stuck in quicksand and had to use the Union Pacific right-of-way through Wyoming, where there was no actual road.

The trip left an impression on Eisenhower, who would spearhead the drive to create the interstate system nearly four decades later.

But Americans wouldn't have to wait that long for better roads. At the end of the First World War, the vast majority of the nation's roadways were still just dirt or gravel, especially in rural areas. In California, work had begun on laying concrete on the Ridge Route across Tehachapi Mountains, which separated the north and southern state, but that process wasn't complete until the end of the century's second decade — and the road was still a perilous, winding two-lane passage across the top of the world. It was also still better than most country roads in the country.

By 1921, however, the federal government had started spending money on highways in a big way. The Federal Highway Act passed that year didn't just set aside a one-time

$75 million sum for road improvement, it budgeted that amount of money *every year*. Within five years, the nation would have its first federal highway system, replacing the privately funded, cobbled-together auto trail network. And by the end of the decade, the government had spent $750 on the nation's roads.

The upshot: There were a lot more miles of (relatively) safe and smooth roads to explore, and American travelers were more than up for the task. Instead of being dropped off at the railroad depot in the center of town, they got behind the wheel and took their itineraries in their own hands. Those railroad depots were near hotels, which had been built specifically to serve the train passengers who disembarked there. They were convenient... if you took the train. This was much less true, however, if you were driving and preferred not to stay overnight in the heart of town.

But the truth was, there wasn't anyplace to stay outside of town — except by the side of the road.

No problem.

A lot of "tin-can tourists" thought it sounded like an adventure: Pack a tent, hook up a trailer, cook out over an open fire and rough it. What could be more fun?

And this was, in fact, the preference of many travelers, as A.L. Westgard revealed in *The Independent* in 1919:

"While hotel accommodations are improving along most routes... more than 50% of the travelers equip themselves more or less elaborately for camping out. Tents, cook stoves, cots, stools and tables are now made light and compact for the use of motorists, and are obtainable in most of the larger cities."

They started off simply stopping by the side of the road along the way, often in farmers' fields. Magazines encouraged this, not only with articles but with ads placed by outdoor companies eager to sell tents, stoves and other items needed for a successful night out under the stars.

The farmers, on the other hand, didn't care much for the trend: Suddenly, they had to deal with litter, abandoned firepits and trespassers picking fruit from their trees. Towns, meanwhile, noticed their shops were losing business to the proponents of these prepackaged vacations. To combat this, they began setting up free makeshift camps just outside their city limits to attract travelers. They offered a clear space to spend the night, perhaps some water and little more. By 1924, some 2,000 free camps had been set up across the country, including one in New York City with room for 1,000 cars. It cost travelers to stay at this one: It offered a restaurant, telephone service, police patrol and a "moving picture display," all within a half-hour of Times Square. Price: $1 for an overnight stay or $5 for a week.

Civic auto camps attracted enough drivers that private landowners started setting up their own rival camps, offering a few basic amenities and eventually building cabins for motorists who didn't want to bring their own tents. By 1929, tent sales had dropped to "normal" levels seen before the start of the auto-camp craze during World War I.

The one-room cabins or bungalows that replaced them weren't anything special. You might expect four walls, a cot and, if you were lucky, a blanket. But modest as they were, these cabins served as the foundation for what would become the modern motel. They offered more privacy, a tad more comfort and more safety: There was a door you could lock to keep undesirables on the other side.

National Parks, a popular tourist destination, also started building cabins.

A row of tourist cabins, later converted into apartments, probably built in the 1920s or '30s along an old alignment of U.S. 101 in Pismo Beach, Calif.

YESTERDAY'S HIGHWAYS

Above: Some old cabin accommodations have remained in use, such as the one in Madera off old U.S. Highway 99 (Gateway Boulevard), which offered adjacent overhangs for cars.

Right: A sign on U.S. 66 in Springfield, Mo., advertises "Modern Cabins" at a place called Graystone Heights. Established in 1935, the motel offered hot and cold running water with private toilets and showers for $1.25 to $1.75 a night. By 1939, the business included eight cabins, a café and a Conoco gas station.

From top: The Shady Rest Motel along old U.S. 101 in San Miguel, Calif., and the Avon, built in 1936 in Afton, Okla., are two examples of cabins at early motels. Just three of the original seven cabins remain at the Avon on Route 66.

Today, Cambria's Bluebird Inn is a home away from home for visitors for California's Central Coast. But it was originally just a *home*. George Lull built it way back in 1881 as a home for his second wife, Mary Inman Lull.

The original home was modified, and additions were made to transform it into a motel. As of 2020, it had six buildings and 37 guest rooms, along with a manager's or owner's quarters.

With all the history behind the Bluebird, it's no surprise that a few visitors have reported bumping into the ghost of Mary Inman over the years. One guest reported getting up in the middle of the night for a walk in the garden and turning at the sound of rustling leaves to see the transparent image of a woman walk *through* the exterior wall and into the Bluebird lounge. She later saw the same image in a mirror.

Motel Inn in San Luis Obispo, Calif., was the first motor court to call itself a motel.

Amenities were added gradually over the years, staring with a few of the basics. Some cabin builders started adding overhangs next to their cabins to protect cars from the elements when they were parked there overnight. And the cabins themselves were often built around central "courts," giving rise to new terms such as "auto court" and "motor court."

The first motel to actually be *called* a motel was the Motel Inn in San Luis Obispo, Calif., which opened in 1925 as the Milestone Mo-Tel alongside the road that would be numbered as U.S. 101 a year later. (See my book *Highway 101* for details.) Other motels, such as the Bakersfield Inn, soon followed, multiplying as the federal highway system came online. Many clustered at the city limits, welcoming motorists with the glow of gaudy signs and neon lights and that formed a sort of entry tunnel to the city proper. If you want to find the template for the Las Vegas strip, look no further than the edge-of-town motel rows that sprang up along America's highways from the 1920s onward.

YESTERDAY'S HIGHWAYS

Clockwise from top right: Neon motel signs beckon travelers at the Western Hills Motel in Flagstaff, Ariz. (Route 66); the Fresno Motel in California (old U.S. 99, now demolished); the Arrowhead Lodge in Gallup, N.M. (Route 66); and the Pony Express in St. Joseph, Mo. (U.S. 29).

Clockwise from top: El Travatore on Route 66 in Kingman, Ariz.; Robbers Roost on U.S. 6/50 in Green River, Utah; and the Stagecoach Motel (featuring Betty Boop) on Route 66 in Seligman, Ariz.

YESTERDAY'S HIGHWAYS

Clockwise from top left: Sky Ranch Motel on Fremont Street/Nevada State Route 582; the Border Motel in Calexico, Calif.; and the Sun 'n Sand off Route 66 in Santa Fe, N.M.

From top: The Western Motel on the Lincoln Highway in North Platte, Neb.; the Grand View Inn on U.S. 52 in South Point, Ohio; and the Starlite Motel on U.S. 36 in Selena, Kan.

YESTERDAY'S HIGHWAYS

Most early motels were mom-and-pop operations. In the auto camp era, travelers back east who didn't want to pitch a tent by the roadside had a more "civilized" option: something called tourist homes. Unlike motels, they were often located in town, but they still offered a more personal, lower-key alternative to the traditional hotel. Homeowners with an extra room or two would move their spare furniture into those spaces and rent them out to road-trippers.

Tourist homes sound a lot like modern bed-and-breakfast arrangements. They often provided meals, just like B&Bs. But they also helped create a template for the first motels, which were often owned by couples or families who put their own distinct stamp on their inns. Tourist homes were each unique simply because they were *homes*; motels, took that distinctiveness even further.

On the open road, it paid to stand out, so motor courts often adopted themes to make themselves more memorable. Images of stars and moons were common, but other motels turned to more specific themes, often with regional hooks. Seaside motels in places like Daytona Beach in Florida and Pismo Beach on California's coast both used the word "Dolphin" in their names. In the desert Southwest, many motels adopted cowboy, Mexican or Native American themes. Names like "Western," "Sands" and "El Rancho," became popular across the region.

The Palomino Motel on Route 66 in Tucumcari, N.M., draws on equine imagery to make a connection with the Old West for the passing motorist.

Clockwise from left: Western-themed motels included the Apache Motel on Route 66 in Tucumcari, N.M.; the Frontier Motel on Truxton, Ariz., on 66; and the Arrow Head Motel on U.S. 40 in Columbia, Mo.

YESTERDAY'S HIGHWAYS

Right: Madonna Inn on U.S. 101 in San Luis Obispo took the themed concept to new heights when it opened in late 1958 with 12 units. Fourteen more rooms were added later, and the inn now features 110 unique guest rooms. Among the themes: Mount Vernon, Pioneer America, Antique Cars, Italy, San Francisco, Caveman, Desert Sands, Showboat, Tack Room and the Highway Suite. Oh, and if you get hungry, there are two restaurants on site, too.

Above: The Dutch Inn in Collinsville, Va., featured a huge windmill that burned down in 2001. But the owners built a new one, seen here. At one time, the motel was part of a chain that included locations in Florida, Puerto Rico, North Carolina, Rhode Island and the nation's capital.

The Art Deco-Streamline Moderne trend, featuring smooth, curved lines, began in the 1930s with motels like Boots Court, built in 1939 along Route 66 in Carthage, Mo., **left and below**. It continued through the '40s, as seen in York, Pa.'s Modernaire Motel, built in 1949 along the Lincoln Highway, **above**. Unlike most Streamline Moderne buildings, the Modernaire made use of brick.

One themed motel concept that really took off was the Wigwam, founded during the Depression by Kentuckian Frank A. Redford. Redford had visited California in 1931, following his father's death, and had been struck by the sight of a concrete roadside eatery called the Tee Pee Barbecue, which had been built in Long Beach a few years earlier.

Redford took the idea to heart in 1933, when he built a teepee-shaped gas station and roadhouse in his hometown. A couple of years later, he added six motel cabins, also shaped like teepees, calling his creation the Wigwam Village. In 1937, he built a second village in Cave City, Ky., with 15 teepee cabins arrayed around a common grassy area.

The villages, with their 32-foot wigwams, were so striking and successful that Redford franchised the idea, and five more teepee-themed motels were eventually built. Three remain standing today: the second one, in Cave City, along with two others farther west — both along old Route 66 — in Holbrook, Ariz. (pictured on previous page) and in San Bernardino, Calif. The first one he built was torn down in 1982.

The Wigwam was ahead of its time in more ways than one. Not only was it a unique visual concept, it was also one of the first motel chains. It was not, however, the largest early chain. That honor went to the Alamo Plaza Hotel Courts, which retained the word "hotel" in its name despite its roadside locations. Originally known as the Alamo Plaza Tourist Apartments, the chain was founded in 1929 by Edgar Lee Torrance in Waco, Texas. The adobe-style façade mimicked that of the Alamo itself, giving the motels a distinctive look that was familiar to drivers looking for a place to spend the night.

The chain soon expanded, with Torrance opening a second location in 1931 in Tyler, Texas, one of only a handful not built on a federal highway. A period of rapid expansion from 1937 to the start of World War II saw about a dozen new motor courts spring up across the South, and by 1950, the chain included locations in Alabama, Arkansas, Georgia, Louisiana, Mississippi, Oklahoma, North Carolina, Texas and Tennessee. One motor court, at the junction of U.S. highways 51 and 80 in Jackson, Miss., was built in 1940 for $100,000 and went included an on-site restaurant called the Plaza Grill. The inn featured a tub or shower/bath, telephone and a "Beautyrest mattress on every bed."

Motels had clearly come a long way in a short span of time.

Alamo cultivated a clean and upscale image, with the restaurant next door offering a fine dining-style menu that featured dishes such as oysters on the half-shell, steak and chops or barbecued chicken. When it came to renting its rooms, the Alamo was particular about its clientele, insisting that this was an "honorable type of operation" that selected "with careful screening, not only its personnel and management, but the type of people permitted to stay" in the establishment. Tourists and business travelers were welcomed; couples with local driver's licenses were turned away. This was *not* a "no-tell motel." Even the tourist court's managers were happily married.

A postcard shows Alamo Plaza Courts in Gulfport, Miss.

To compete with Alamo — and to increase their own business footprint — other motels began to form associations, which offered referrals from one motel to others in the cooperative. The motels all had different owners; it was a "you scratch my back, I'll scratch yours" type of arrangement, with members agreeing to meet certain standards in order to be part of the network. Identifying shields were hung outside each member motel, and pamphlets available at each location contained information on (and directions to) others in the system.

One of the first, United Motor Courts, was formed in 1933 in Santa Barbara, Calif., by "a friendly group of independent owners of motor lodges." According to *The Saturday Evening Post*, the network was the brainchild of Oscar and Walton Tomerlin, owners of the Bakersfield Inn. The brothers "decided that something ought to be done to lift motor courts out of the campground status," so they invited several other owners to a meeting. Among them: "Harvey Coons, of Long Beach; George Anderson, of Merced; the Grosset brothers, of Stockton; (and) the Hamiltons, of San Luis Obispo."

Together with some others, they formed the UMC, collecting fees to hire inspectors who would ensure each motel's rooms were clean, its beds were comfortable, and its service was acceptable. Using the slogan "For surpassing comfort," UMC grew into the largest nonprofit motor court network during the prewar years.

Similar nonprofit groups followed: Quality Courts United was born from a group of seven Florida motor court owners in 1939; Best Western Motels arrived in 1947; and Superior Courts United was organized in 1950. Meanwhile, franchise chains such as Travelodge (1939) and Holiday Inn (1952) were emerging.

When it was founded, Best Western entered into a partnership with Quality Courts: The two weren't competitors, since Best Western operated mostly west of the Mississippi, while Quality Courts was concentrated in the East, so they shared referrals for travelers heading from one region to the other. This lasted until the early 1960s, at which point Quality Courts became a for-profit entity and Best Western expanded nationwide, becoming a chain in its own right. (It briefly had a "Best Eastern" brand, which it ultimately dropped.) Quality Courts eventually morphed into Choice Hotels, parent of Quality Inn, Econo Lodge, Rodeway Inn, Clarion Hotels and several others.

As of 2019, Best Western had 4,500 hotels worldwide, while Choice boasted 7,005 franchise properties in 41 countries.

A vintage postcard displays Holiday Inn's iconic sign. The chain took its name from the popular Christmas movie of the same name starring Bing Crosby and Bob Hope.

YESTERDAY'S HIGHWAYS

Laura Lodge on U.S. 101 in Santa Maria retains the iconic sign from its days as a Travelodge, with the first word altered to fit the new owner's identity, and minus the sleepwalking Sleepy Bear that serves as the Travelodge mascot. The bear in nightshirt and nightcap dates to 1954.

The expansion of chain motels has come largely at the expense of the mom-and-pop operations that kicked off the movement in the 1920s and '30s. More than 200 motels were built in the first nine months of 1960, and four years later, there were 61,000 motels along America's highways.

The chains kept right on growing, with Holiday Inn reaching 568 franchises by 1966, but like gas stations, the industry as a whole went into decline, with the vast majority of independent operators giving up the ghost. By 2012, only about 16,000 motels were still in business nationwide. But they didn't just disappear — at least not all of them.

If you drive along an old federal highway, you'll see plenty of old motel signs still standing next to vacant lots filled with weeds poking up through cracked concrete. Most motels were built cheaply and weren't intended to last more than about a decade, so many were demolished once they'd served their purpose.

A sign for the Apple Valley Motel on Route 66 north of St. Louis is decorated with holiday lights and still alerts truck drivers to its "circle drive." But there's nothing there except a vacant lot.

Others, though, continued to linger. Owners improved profitable sites, but those that failed were abandoned or converted into monthly rentals for low-income residents.

In some cities, those glowing and glittering neon "welcome tunnels" became dark and dingy dens of crime, drug use and prostitution in the second half of the 20th century — especially on highways bypassed by Eisenhower's interstates. In Fresno, Calif., the once vibrant "motel row" that had been part of old Highway 99 became a red-light district after that section of road was bypassed by a new, wider freeway that paralleled the old road to the west. Motel Drive, as it was rechristened, had once been the northern gateway to the city, lined with fine establishments like the Fresno Motel, Town House Motel and, farther north, the Astro. By the late 20th century, they were shadows of their former selves. Ultimately, they were torn down to make way for a rail project.

The old southern gateway to the city went downhill for the same reason. Vintage motor courts such as The Gables, Big Star and The City limped along, consigned to a mostly neglected section of road away from the modern highway.

Elsewhere, entire towns vanished completely, taking their motel rows with them. Places like Texola on the Texas-Oklahoma state line and Glenrio, where Texas meets New Mexico, became ghost towns when Route 66 was replaced by Interstate 40. Their motels, gas stations, cafés and other travel-oriented businesses closed, leaving skeletons of decaying buildings alongside empty stretches of road.

YESTERDAY'S HIGHWAYS

Top: The Texas Longhorn Motel in Glenrio, Texas, opened in 1955, two years after the adjacent State Line Café and Gas Station, which dispensed Phillips 66. One side of the sign said "First Stop in Texas"; the other said "Last Stop in Texas." The bar was in New Mexico because Texas was dry; the gas was sold in Texas, because taxes were lower there. **Above:** "Modern Restrooms" sign in Glenrio.

The Gardenway Motel, built in 1945, featured 41 rooms with tile baths and a huge sign on Route 66 in Villa Ridge, Mo., that made it hard to miss. It closed without warning in 2014 after seven decades in business, all under the same family ownership.

YESTERDAY'S HIGHWAYS

From top: All that's left of the Tumble Inn, built in the 1920s on the Ridge Route in California; the Franciscan Lodge ("Your Home on the Road") on Route 66 in Grants, N.M.; the closed Piedras Blancas Motel north of Cambria, Calif., on the Pacific Coast Highway.

Route 66 through the Mojave Desert in California is largely a ghost road today, veering away from Interstate 40 at Ludlow and heading through former highway stops like Bagdad, Amboy and Chambless that are now little more than memories. Once, there were places to stay in the desert; now, with very few exceptions, there are only skeletal signs. Today, the two motel signs shown here stand all by themselves in the desert.

Roadside Attractions

Ride on the Weird Side

From bowling alleys to parks, from theaters to zoos to miniature golf, the American roadside has long been fertile ground for attractions — tourist and otherwise. There's plenty to do, and plenty to see along the highway.

Take, for example, the Blue Whale of Catoosa, seen above along Route 66 in Oklahoma. Hugh Davis built the whale next to a pond on his property in 1972: It was a 34th anniversary gift to his wife, Zelta, who collected whale figurines. Davis had already built a couple of petting zoos, one for cats and the other containing reptiles, which he dubbed the "Animal Reptile Kingdom" — ARK, for short.

You can still walk through the whale's mouth and onto its tail, which serves as a dock from which young swimmers once jumped in for a dip or climbed down a stepladder into the pond. If fishing's your thing, you can cast a line into the water. Picnic tables are also available, along with a small gift shop stocked with souvenirs.

Along U.S. 11, the Lee Highway in Virginia, there's a similarly kitschy stop called Dinosaur Kingdom II in Natural Bridge. The natural bridge itself is an attraction in its own right. The 215-foot-tall stone "bridge" is actually a limestone gorge carved by Cedar Creek on land once owned by Thomas Jefferson.

The Dinosaur Kingdom is less natural, and in fact features a bizarre historical mashup of prehistoric predators and Civil War figures. A Confederate soldier duels with a T-Rex atop a train at the park's entrance (see photo on next page). A Union soldier sits in the jaws of a dinosaur. A figure "milks" a stegosaurus in a shed as if it's a cow. A union soldier supervises a game of tug-of-war between a crested dino and a baby stegosaurus. A velociraptor stalks Abe Lincoln.

The original attraction, inspired by a 1969 movie called *The Valley of Gwangii*, was destroyed in a 2012 fire, along with a Monster Museum next door. But owner Mark Cline rebuilt it and opened a new version in 2016.

The backstory of the place is told on a plaque at the park entrance:

> "It's mid-June, 1864. General David Hunter has just raided and burned nearby Lexington and has continued maneuvering his troops toward Lynchburg. Several Union scouts have detoured near Natural Bridge and have discovered their recent cannon fire has awakened **PREHISTORIC CREATURES** who have been cryogenically hibernating in a lost section of the Natural Bridge Caverns for Millions of years. An idea forms to use these giant reptiles as **WEAPONS OF MASS DESTRUCTION** against the South. But you will soon see that not everything goes as planned!"

Other bits of the tale can be found inside the park, such as the story of Professor Cline, who needs "massive amounts of gold" to fuel his time machine and starts searching for a buried treasure. Gen. Stonewall Jackson, meanwhile, races to beat him to the prize.

YESTERDAY'S HIGHWAYS

Dinosaurs aren't the only things you'll find at Dinosaur Kingdom II. There are other huge sculptures in evidence, too, such as these: One looks like a giant tick; the other resembles a stylized pharaoh's face.

YESTERDAY'S HIGHWAYS

Dinosaur Kingdom II is hardly the only prehistory attraction along the roadside. In fact, it may sometimes seem there are more dinos along the side of the modern highway than there were roaming the landscape in the Jurassic Period. Following are just a few of the sights you'll see by the roadside.

A brontosaurus named "Zoomie" and some hungry predators stand guard over an old miniature golf course outside a motel at Grand Canyon Caverns on Route 66.

Above: The Cabazon Dinosaurs roam the Earth beside Interstate 10 in Southern California. Sculptor Claude Bell began work on Dinny, the brontosaurus, in 1964 and completed him in 1975 — the same year he started work on a companion, Mr. Rex (which he finished in 1981). The gigantic dinosaurs were built to attract travelers to Bell's Wheel Inn Café, next door.

Below: A raptor stalks a teepee on Route 66 at the Painted Desert Indian Center.

YESTERDAY'S HIGHWAYS

Top and left: Dinosaurs call attention to Stewart's Petrified Wood on Route 66 in Holbrook, Ariz.

Above: A van outfitted to look like a triceratops is parked outside Dinosaur Journey museum, off U.S. 50 and Interstate 70 in Fruita, Colo.

Roadside attractions are a hodgepodge of kitsch and wonder. At the Mystery Spot in Santa Cruz, Calif., a youngster can stand at one end of a room and appear taller than his dad at the other. Balls seem to roll uphill. You can apparently lean far forward without falling on your face. George Prather opened the attraction in 1939, and visitors have marveled at the optical illusions ever since.

Confusion Hill, which opened ten years later on U.S. 101 in Piercy, Calif., featured a "gravity house" that produced similar optical illusions, along with a train ride and other attractions.

Some of the sights at Confusion Hill, founded in 1949 along U.S. 101 in Northern California. The Redwood Shoe House, above, began as a float in a local parade in 1947. The Mountain Train Ride runs 1¼ miles over a 20-guage track to the hilltop and back.

YESTERDAY'S HIGHWAYS

Confusion Hill also features what it calls the world's largest freestanding redwood chainsaw carving, a totem pole in the parking lot that was carved out of a dead tree in 1992. It took three months to create the sculpture, which rises 40 feet above the ground. It's one of numerous world's largest (fill in the blank) attractions that have popped up beside America's highways over the years.

Among them, the "world's largest":

- Thermometer off Interstate 15 in Baker, Calif., between Los Angeles and Las Vegas. It really bakes in Baker: It gets mighty hot in the desert there.
- Basket on Main Street in Newark, Ohio, is really a seven-story building that serves as headquarters for the Longaberger Basket Co.
- Corn dog on top of the Original Pronto Pup restaurant in Rockaway Beach, Ore. — the town where the confection was invented in the 1930s.
- Strawberry in Ellerbe, N.C.: a strawberry-shaped building not unlike the Giant Oranges from California, which dispenses ice cream next to a vegetable stand. It's 24 feet tall.
- Light bulb, in Edison, N.J., near Thomas Edison's former lab. At 13 feet tall, it stands at the apex of a 12-story Art Deco tower and weighs some eight tons.
- Fork, weighing more than 600 pounds. This aluminum utensil fit for the Jolly Green Giant is off Highway 149 at the Cascada Bar and Grill in Creed, Colo.

That's just the short list. In fact, several sites have vied for the title of "world's largest" this or that over the years. No fewer than six claimants have purported to have the world's largest frying pan. The world's largest chair? It might be in Alabama, in Binghamton, N.Y., or somewhere else, depending whom you ask.

Two rivals — Minnesota farmer Frank Johnson and Kansas resident Frank Stoeber — vied for years to create the world's largest ball of twine. Johnson got started in 1950, and Stoeber began his quest three years later, outdoing his opponent to be recognized by the Guinness Book of World Records in 1973. Johnson didn't quit, though. Stoeber died in 1974, but Johnson kept on winding that yarn 'round and 'round until *his* ball was recognized by Guinness in 1979. By the time of Johnson's death in 1989, he'd been going for nearly four decades, spinning a yarn ball 12 feet wide and weighing 17,400 pounds.

The World's Largest Catsup Bottle (they spell it with a "C," not a "K") is actually a water tower built in 1949 that rises 170 feet over Route 159 in Collinsville, Ill. It's one of several water towers dressed up to look like various objects across the country.

Left: A teapot water tower stands off Highway 99 in Kingsburg, Calif.

Below: A smiley face adorns a water tower in Atlanta, Ill., off Route 66.

YESTERDAY'S HIGHWAYS

Size is the common denominator. Indeed, one thing many roadside attractions have in common is that they're larger than life — even if they're alive, like the Chandelier Tree off old U.S. 101 in the Northern California town of Leggett. The tree, pictured below, is more than 275 feet high and 16 feet wide. That's wide enough to allow a car to drive through a tunnel in its base, which was carved out in the 1930s.

The Chandelier Tree in Leggett and the Grandfather Tree in Piercy are two of several redwood-based attractions in Northern California.

The area is known for its giant redwoods, so it's no surprise that a series of tree-based attractions in the area: They include the quirky One-Log House in Garberville, the 1,800-year-old Grandfather Tree in Piercy, the Redwood Tree Service Station in Ukiah, and the Trees of Mystery in Klamath — which dates from 1946. Billing itself as the "premier nature attraction on California's North Coast," it features giant 49- and 35-foot-high statues of Paul Bunyan and Babe the Blue Ox. The pair weigh in at 30,000 pounds each.

Bunyan and Babe are among the most massive roadside statues out there, but they're far from the only ones. Some of the most common are the "muffler men" — who in fact started out as Paul Bunyan statues themselves. Each one is molded in the same stance: feet spread wide apart; arms bent at the elbows and hands held out in front of him just above the waist, as if holding something.

Since he was Paul Bunyan, the archetypal lumberjack, that "something" was originally an ax. The first of the fiberglass figures was created in 1962 to stand outside the Flagstaff, Ariz., Paul Bunyan Café on Route 66. But the way the hands were positioned meant they could hold a variety of different things, from golf clubs to giant hot dogs. A large number of them stood outside auto shops and held mufflers, accounting for why they came to be called muffler men. But quite a few others were attired in various ways to promote various different products. Here's just a sampling.

- "Giant Chip," with an ice cream cone in one hand and a scooper in the other, at the Inside Scoop ice cream parlor about 40 miles north of Philadelphia.
- "Casino Dude," attired in a cowboy hat and holding a rifle, outside the Rockvale Restaurant and Casino in Joliet, Mont.
- "El Salsero," adorned in a sombrero and holding a taco platter atop a Mexican restaurant on the Pacific Coast Highway in Malibu, Calif. The place used to be a burger joint, and the statue once held a hamburger.
- "Chicken Boy," on Route 66 in Highand Park, Calif. The statue's head was changed to that of a chicken, and the arms were repositioned to hug a bucket of chicken.
- "Greg E. Normous," named for golfer Greg Norman, who stands at a miniature golf course in New Baltimore, Mich. Instead of a muffler, he holds a putter.

YESTERDAY'S HIGHWAYS

A couple of muffler men stand along Route 66 in Illinois.

Above: A giant hot dog statue in Atlanta, Ill., originally stood at Bunyon's restaurant in Cicero, Ill.

Right: The Gemini Giant in Wilmington, Ill., was decked out in a space suit and given a rocket to hold outside the Launching Pad Drive-in. The Giant was named for the Gemini space program.

Not, she's not dancing to Elvis' music. The figure above, stands off U.S. 395 at Hubcap World in Pearsonville, Calif. Elvis, meanwhile, is "in concert" at the Polk-a-Dot Drive Inn on Route 66 in Braidwood, Ill. The woman was a "Uniroyal Gal," the female counterpart to the Muffler Man.

YESTERDAY'S HIGHWAYS

Clockwise from top: The five-story Haines Shoe House, built by a shoe salesman in 1948 on the Lincoln Highway in Pennsylvania; Daniel Boone on North Carolina Route 86; a teapot house at Mr. Ed's Elephant Museum on the Lincoln Highway.

Roadside attractions over the years have ranged from the whimsical to the wacky. Once upon a time, you could stop at the themed Santa Claus Lane off U.S. 101 in California for a taste of Christmas all year 'round. (The buildings are still there, as is the street name, but the attraction is long gone.) You can still visit Mr. Ed's Elephant Museum on the Lincoln Highway in Pennsylvania and see more than 12,000 elephant figures, big and small, while sampling a few of the candy store's 100 flavors of fudge.

You might stop at retail attractions like Bravo Farms on Interstate 5 or Highway 99 in California, with its Old West façades on the outside and plenty of food, diversions and vintage collectibles. Or at the similarly expansive Uranus in Missouri on Route 66, which sells fudge alongside souvenirs heavy on double-entendres, and offers activities ranging from axe throwing to a tattoo studio amid dozens of props: dinosaurs, vintage vehicles, a rocket ship...

Some of what you'll see at Uranus, Mo., founded in 2015 off Route 66: a rocket ship and a dinosaur (appearing to eat a passing car on the highway). There's also a vintage police car, a double-decker bus, a vintage water tower and plenty of other things to see.

YESTERDAY'S HIGHWAYS

An 18-foot tall St. Nick once gazed down on Santa Claus Lane from a huge chimney above this complex near Oxnard, Calif. The attraction started as a juice stand called the North Pole in 1948, then grew to include a candy store, toy store, magic shop, Santa's Kitchen pie shop, a kids' train and a giant Frosty the Snowman.

The self-proclaimed World's Largest Gift Store along Route 66 in Phillipsburg, Mo., includes an exhibit of the 1940 Cadillac used in the *I Love Lucy* TV show.

Left and below: Teepee Curios on Route 66 in Tucumcari, N.M.

Bottom: The Fort Courage attraction on Route 66 in Houck, Ariz., was based on the 1960s TV comedy *F-Troop*. As of 2019, it was abandoned and up for sale.

YESTERDAY'S HIGHWAYS

Above: A plane appears to have crashed into a Delaware diner in this 1939 photo. *Library of Congress*

Left: The ultimate roadside attraction? Mount Rushmore. Here, two workers put some finishing touches on George Washington's face in this 1932 photo. *Library of Congress*

Top: A weird head recalls Easter Island on Route 66 in Van Wert, Ariz.

Left: A tribute to James Dean at Blackwell's Corners on State Route 46 in California.

Roadside Recreation
Have Fun, Will Travel

Celebration Station in Greensboro, N.C., is part of a small chain with locations in Louisiana, Texas, Florida and Oklahoma. The miniature golf craze began in the 1920s, but later courses were often part of "fun centers" that also featured such attractions as pizza parlors, video arcades and bumper cars.

Not all roadside attractions were stocked with candy or supersized ice cream cones. Some provided big-screen entertainment, and others, like miniature golf and bowling, were even (surprise) healthy.

The popularity of theaters along the highway hearkens back to a time when major roads ran *through* towns, not around them.

Many sit-down theaters were built along highways in the center of town, where roads like the Lincoln Highway were known as Main Street or Broadway. Drive-ins, meanwhile, went up on highways near the outskirts of town — just far enough away to insulate quiet neighborhoods from the bright lights of the theater and the hubbub of young patrons coming and going in their Mustangs and Corvairs.

In the 1970s, stately downtown theaters would begin giving way to multiplexes in the suburbs, while drive-ins would start closing down near the end of the decade. The number of drive-ins peaked at 4,000 in the late '50s, but had declined to just 321 by the time 2019 rolled around.

At one time in the '70s, Martinsville, Va. had no fewer than four drive-ins — three of them within a couple of square miles off U.S. Highway 220 — serving a population of fewer than 20,000 people. All four of those closed in the late '70s and '80s, although a single drive-in soldiered on a half-hour south in Eden, N.C.

Eden Drive-In opened in 1949 with room for 200 cars off North Carolina State Route 770. It remained open 70 years later.

YESTERDAY'S HIGHWAYS

Top: The Van-Del Drive-In opened in the summer of 1948 on the Lincoln Highway in Middle Point, Ohio. It was known as the Star Lite back then and became Staup's Auto Movie the following year. It remained open in 2019.
Above: The Valley Drive-in in Lompoc on the Pacific Coast Highway is closed.

From top: The still-open Sunset in San Luis Obispo, Calif., on U.S. 101; the long-closed Moon-Glo on old U.S. 99, Fresno; the Valley Drive-In on U.S. 6 in Fort Morgan, Colo.; and the closed Rt. 52 Flying Saucer Drive-In (now an auto parts place), Cincinnati.

Photographs taken by John Margolies between 1979 and 1981 document now-vanished Southern California drive-in theaters that used the backs of their screens as self-promoting billboards. The Van Nuys and San Pedro drive-ins both featured riders on horseback, while the Lakewood Drive-In depicted sailboats riding the ocean waves. *Library of Congress photos*

Drive-ins — and later, multiplexes — were successors to the opulent theaters that appeared during the roaring twenties where highways passed through bustling downtown retail districts. Big theaters with plenty of seats and luxurious fixtures became a symbol of American abundance in the years leading up to the Great Depression. Balconies, chandeliers, red velvet curtains and intricate molding were the rule of the day. They were, indeed, *theaters*, not just cinemas, meant to resemble opera houses, with impressive names like the Orpheum, the Hippodrome, the Roxy and the Ritz.

In the days of silent film, they had orchestra pits and grand organs to provide a suitable soundtrack to the action on the screen. Many still hosted live performances, in addition to film screenings, and they most certainly did *not* serve popcorn, soda or candy in their lobbies. The plush seats weren't designed to be spilled upon; besides, the theater was serious business, which commanded one's complete attention.

Major film producers built their "palaces" to solidify their brand and impress patrons. The so-called Big Five studios (MGM, Paramount, Fox, RKO and Warner Bros.) raked in nearly three-quarters of everything spent at the box office by the end of the 1920s. Paramount owned 1,200 theaters nationwide, and Fox operated 1,100 more.

Major cities like Chicago and Los Angeles had them; so did smaller towns like Dunsmuir, Calif. Many of the ornate theaters featured columns and arches in the European style. Grauman's Chinese in Hollywood (which opened in 1927 with the premiere of Cecil B. DeMille's epic *The King of Kings* and also hosted the premier of *Star Wars* a half-century later), featured an Asian motif. The East Indian-themed Oriental Theatre in Milwaukee opened the same year.

Kansas City's Main Street theater debuted in 1921, with 3,000 seats and a basement roomy enough to house cages for animals — including elephants — used in vaudeville shows. That was the same year the Chicago Theatre opened, touting itself as the "Wonder of the Theatre World" with nearly 3,900 seats. Ronald Reagan would announce his engagement to first wife Jane Wyman there.

Fresno, Calif., had several downtown theaters and was the second West Coast city to boast a Warner Bros. theater. It opened in 1928 as the Pantages, part of a chain owned by Alexander Pantages; Warner Bros. bought it the following year. A 1948 court decision forced the studios to divest themselves of their properties, and the theater was eventually renamed the Warnors to avoid trademark issues.

YESTERDAY'S HIGHWAYS

Top and right: Views outside and inside the Warnors Theatre in Fresno, Calif., which opened in 1928 as the Pantages. **Above:** The Wilson, just down the street from the Warnors, opened in 1925 and featured a Wurlitzer organ.

Left: The Chicago was the flagship of the Balaban and Katz chain, which operated 28 theaters in the city and more than 100 in the Midwest. It featured a Wurlitzer organ and a 50-piece orchestra.

Right: The 1,200-seat Missouri Theater in St. Joseph opened in 1927 with a screening of the silent film *Rough House Rosie*. Admission: 25 cents.

A 6,000-light sign overlooks Broadway in Portland, Ore., outside a theater that opened in the spring of 1928 as the Portland Publix Theatre. The a $1.5 million, 3,036-seat auditorium featured a $46,500 Wurlitzer organ and was the work of Chicago architects George and Cornelius Rapp, designers of more than 400 theaters. Part of the nearly 2,000-screen Publix chain, it became known as the Portland Paramount in 1930; it's now a performing arts venue.

Right: The Spanish-Moorish-style Tennessee Theatre in Knoxville was touted as "the South's most beautiful theatre" when it opened in 1928. It features French-style chandeliers with Czechoslovakian crystals, and Italian terrazzo flooring in the lobby.

Below: The Coleman Theatre in Miami, Okla., hailed as the most elaborate entertainment venue between Dallas and Kansas City. It was built in 1929 for local mining magnate George Coleman, who wanted a big-city theater for locals and travelers along Route 66.

YESTERDAY'S HIGHWAYS

The ornate movie palaces of the 1920s gave way, over the next two decades, to sleek Art Deco movie houses.

The term "Art Deco" wasn't actually used to describe the style until the 1960s, but the style is unmistakable: clean lines and smooth, flowing surfaces. Its big, bold ornamentation contrasts with the highly detailed, intricate surfaces of the Victorian age. It overlaps with a style known as "Moderne," whose teardop lines grew out of the idea that curved surfaces cut down on wind resistance.

Not surprisingly, when the concept took hold on the highway, it wasn't just in theaters (and diners and billboards), but in the cars themselves. In the 1930s, carmakers started producing models with lines that looked like swirls of cloud or waves on the ocean: the 1933 Cadillac V-16 Aerod-Dynamic Coupe, the '33 Pierce Arrow and the '34 Hudson Eight Special, to name a few.

When drivers passed theaters built in this new style, they saw a reflection of the cars they'd chosen: modern, sleek, and full of hope and promise.

The Mexico Theatre on a stretch of old U.S. 101 in San Jose opened as the Mayfair, an Art Deco movie house, in 1949 with 600 seats.

The Fremont on old U.S. 101 in San Luis Obispo, Calif., exhibits the curved, swirling lines of the Art Deco style in its sign and in the patterns on the ceiling in its exterior lobby (inset).

Art Deco marquees in California, **clockwise from top left**: The Star in Oceanside, which opened in 1956; the Fortuna in (naturally) Fortuna, built for the Redwood Theatre chain in 1938; and the Crest in Fresno, which dates from 1949. The Star and Fortuna were both built along old U.S. 101, while the Crest stands along old U.S. 99.

Stretching Your Legs

If you'd driven a long way on the highway, the last thing you'd probably want to do is spend even *more* time sitting — either in your car at a drive-in or in a movie palace, no matter how comfortable. But there were options that involved actually getting your legs moving and your heart pumping.

Were you really adventurous? You could always lace on some skates: the kind with wheels or the kind with blades.

During the first half of the 20th century, roller skating was a pastime pursued in buildings that doubled as ballrooms and music halls. But the same postwar road boom that spurred the construction of drive-ins and bowling alleys around the country saw scores of new roller rinks appear by the roadside.

When the Route 66 Roller Dome in Sapulpa, Okla., opened in 1951, it was known as the Starlite Skate Center. It closed in 2002, then reopened in 2011 under its current name.

When a 200-foot-long rink in Levittown, N.Y., opened in 1955, it drew throngs of up to 1,750 kids on a Friday night. The rink was torn down in the 1980s, but another vintage site — Moonlight Rollerway in Glendale, Calif. — was still in business as of 2020. The rink opened in 1950 in a building that had been used for airplane foundry parts. The owner, Harry Dickerman, transformed it into one of several Harry's Roller Rinks he operated in Southern California.

YESTERDAY'S HIGHWAYS

Top: The Ontario Ice Skating Center offered cold comfort along the hot highway (U.S. 99, now Holt Boulevard) starting in 1957.

Above: The Roll-A-Bout Skating Center put wheels on customers' feet in Collinsville, Va., from 1983 to 2019.

Across the country, roller rinks popped up with names like:

- Rollercade (1959) off U.S. Highway 281 in San Antonio.
- Nampa Rollerdome (1948) in Nampa, Idaho, near the Lincoln Highway.
- Skateland in Bakersfield, Calif. (1955), about a mile off U.S. 99.
- Roll-A-Bout Skating Center (1983) off U.S. 220 in Collinsville, Va.
- Starlite Skate Center (1951), now the Route 66 Roller Dome in Sapulpa, Okla.

Roll-A-Bout was one of four locations in a small chain — the others being in Asheboro, Burlington and Eden, N.C. Michael Foley owned the Roll-A-Bout from the time it opened until his death in 2016; he even met his wife Christia there. She continued to operate the Collinsville location until the end of 2019, when she decided to scale back operations by closing it. (The Eden and Burlington locations remained open).

Ice skating was another option, in places like Icelandia, off old Highway 99 in Fresno, and the Ontario Ice Center in Southern California, off Holt Avenue, another old alignment of U.S. 99.

If balancing on a pair of skates wasn't your thing, but you still wanted a bit of exercise, you could always try bowling or miniature golf. The two pastimes both became popular at stops along highways before the era of the interstate. Miniature golf got its start in Tennessee, where Garnet Carter bought 700 acres of land at Lookout Mountain in the 1920s.

Carter had an inn there, and he wanted to build an exclusive subdivision there that would include a golf course. His wife, meanwhile, created a rock garden decorated with statues of fairytale characters she dubbed Fairyland. It was a concept that converged with Carter's golf course plans to create a new phenomenon.

Carter announced plans for his full-scale course in the 1920s, but ran into problems that delayed construction; meanwhile, would-be golfers were clamoring for a place to play. He had to do something. So, to appease them, he set up a small putting course in 1927. It wasn't the first "miniature" golf course, but it was different than executive or pitch-and-putt courses, which were just scaled-back versions of a regulation layout. Carter's course featured his wife's Fairyland statues and, in an effort to make it more challenging, he added obstacles such as pieces of pipe, tile, rock tunnels and logs.

YESTERDAY'S HIGHWAYS

Top: A 20-foot-tall gold prospector (originally part of the annual Grass Valley Forty-Niners parade) stands guard over the Mallard Lake Golf Center near Yuba City on old U.S. 99E. **Above and right:** The Laurel Park Mini Golf Course on U.S. 58 east of Martinsville, Va., featured a basic layout and lots of lights for night play.

Tiny Town Golf on Arnett Boulevard in Danville, Va., opened in 1965. After being closed for several years, it reopened under new management in 2018, charging the same prices it had 20 years earlier: $6.50 for adults or $5.50 for children, seniors and groups playing a full 18 holes. Among the obstacles: the infamous windmill stands at the ready to knock your best shot off course.

YESTERDAY'S HIGHWAYS

The course was a hit, not only with golfers waiting for the "main course," but with guests at his inn and others who drove up to Lookout Mountain based on word of mouth. Carter eventually built his regulation course, but his Tom Thumb Golf (as he called it) was even more popular. Carter responded by building similar courses across the South, and the idea truly became a craze. In August of 1930, just three years after Carter opened his first course, the Department of Commerce estimated that 25,000 tiny courses were operating across the country — 15,000 of which had opened just since the beginning of the year.

As many as 2 or 3 million people were playing every day.

"The total investment represented is probably around $75,000,000," *Popular Mechanics* reported. "Vacant lots have been snatched up everywhere. Signboards have been torn down; auto parking spaces have been taken over. New York jokesters even tell the story that an attempt was made to buy a famous hotel, with the idea of razing it to make room for a miniature golf course."

The magazine described the typical course as par 42 or 43, but "usually there is no hole that cannot be made in one if the ball is hit correctly — and the player is lucky."

The number of courses had grown to 40,000 by World War II, but the craze petered out during the war and faced new competition afterward. Suddenly, there were skating rinks, regional malls, bowling alleys, drive-ins and, at home, a newfangled contraption called a television. But Ralph and Al Lomma, two brothers from Scranton, Pa., emerged to revitalize the business in 1955. They added a new wrinkle to their courses in the form of motorized obstacles such as windmills, which could knock even a well-struck ball away at the last moment if the player's timing was off. Another innovation: Players could win a free game by hitting a clown's nose with the ball on the final hole, after which the balls were gobbled up and the game was over.

The Lommas' innovations were so successful, they became the largest manufacturers of miniature golf courses, with more than 5,000 worldwide. Miniature golf courses (the preferred term, having eclipsed Tom Thumb, putt-putt and midget golf) can be found all over. There's Skyline Mini Golf on the roof of an art museum in Minneapolis, and a glow-in-the-dark indoor course called Main Event in Columbia, Md. Can Can Wonderland in St. Paul, Minn., is inside an old can factory. But many miniature golf courses are still found by the side of the road, along America's highways.

The same can be said for bowling centers, which exploded in popularity after World War II, spurred in part by the addition of automatic pinsetters. No longer did bowlers have to wait for a "pin boy" to manually reset the pins after each frame; now, there was a motorized gizmo to do it for them.

More than 20,000 lanes were built between 1945 and 1957, and local bowling league results became a staple of the sports pages.

By the mid-1960s, there were 12,000 bowling centers in the United States. Fred and Barney hit the bowling alley on *The Flintstones*. The Pro Bowlers Tour was on TV every Saturday afternoon, when ABC and announcer Chris Schenkel brought tournaments into America's living room from cities like Toledo, Akron, Fresno, Kansas City and Fort Smith, Ark. There was even a short-lived National Bowling League that aimed to pattern itself after Major League Baseball. (For more, see my book *A Whole Different League*.)

Like drive-in theaters, however, bowling alleys went into a slow decline in the 1980s and onward, with the number of sites dwindling to fewer than 4,000 by 2015. Fewer people were signing up for leagues, but another reason for the decline may have been the change in American's highways, with bypasses and interstates funneling drivers past the old roadside centers. Many, like Mid-State Bowl in Fresno, were torn down; others were left vacant; still others were converted to other uses.

Still, many bowling alleys survive along the highway, not just as a reminder of yesteryear but as a destination for modern motorists, as well.

A bowling center on the Lincoln Highway in Massillon, Ohio.

YESTERDAY'S HIGHWAYS

Above: Surf Bowl in Oceanside opened as a 10-lane bowling alley, adding six lanes in 1964 and 16 more in 1976. It's been known at various times as Welcome Lanes and Bowl-O-Rama. These days, it offers glow-in-the-dark bowling, among other attractions.

Right: Sportlanes in Collinsville, Va., opened in 1962 in a converted Chrysler building on U.S. 220. It also has a café and is known for its Sportlanes Burger.

From top: A giant bowling pin on Route 66 in southwestern Missouri; Star-Way Lanes near Massillon, Ohio, on the Lincoln Highway; Eastridge Lanes on Route 66 east of Amarillo.

Signs and Billboards

A billboard for Pea Soup Andersen's along U.S. 101 north of Buellton.

Big Ads

It didn't take long for advertisers realized one thing about drivers: Whether their engines were idling at a city intersection or they were chugging along on a country road, they were a captive audience. In the days before the internet, television or even radio, there weren't many opportunities, beyond word of mouth, to spread the news about their products. But the open road offered them an almost limitless canvas on which to paint their pitches, prices and slogans. So, they did.

Much as the first road signs were painted or tacked up on fence posts and phone poles, the rural billboard was born on the sides of brick buildings, wagons and barns. Circus posters started a trend toward larger visual ads in the 1830s, and by 1870, there were nearly 300 companies painting signs and posting bills, as they were called. Areas to be kept free of such ads were labeled with a warning to "post no bills." Boards where they were permitted were "bill-boards."

Ever wonder how Billboard Magazine, which tracks the popularity of music in America, got its name? It started out as a trade publication for billboard companies. Some of the earliest billboards were in railyards and train depots, situated to give passengers a good look as trains pulled slowly into the station.

On the open road, two different sorts of billboards popped up. Some ads touted general products that could be purchased later on, while others related directly to destinations along the road. Because drivers were approaching from farther away, and faster, than observers in the center of town, the ads had to be bigger and bolder than the small circulars on a downtown bill-board. That's why many early advertisers put signs on the sides of buildings or barns.

The most famous of these were the Mail Pouch Tobacco signs that began appearing in the Ohio Valley and nearby in 1896. Company owners Aaron and Samuel Bloch had the idea of paying farmers an annual fee for the right to use their barns. For $1 to $10 a year, they'd provide a paint job and minor repairs before creating a huge billboard in block lettering on the side facing the road. Mail Pouch ads went up thousands of times in the century that followed, and their famous gold block letters against a black or red background invited passing motorists to "Treat yourself to the best."

At their peak in the 1960s, there were 20,000 Mail Pouch barn signs in 22 states.

Sign painters made an interesting living. When Harley Warrick got back from the Army in 1946, he found a Mail Pouch crew painting his family's barn. They told him they were looking for more painters, and he accepted the job after deciding it was better than milking cows. Working for $32 a week, to start, he spent the next 45 years repainting up to six barns a day in 13 states from New York to Missouri. A paint job would last four or five years before it needed to be touched up. By the time he retired in 1993, he'd painted some 20,000 barns by eyeballing them, starting with the "E" in "CHEW."

Some remain visible today, in various states of repair. Some letters on rotting and abandoned barns are fading, nearly beyond recognition, while others are lovingly maintained by barn owners as a tribute to an earlier time. There's even a Mail Pouch sign on a private covered bridge in Guernsey County, Ohio, off Route 146. The bridge was built in 1981, so the sign isn't that old, but it certainly is unique.

YESTERDAY'S HIGHWAYS

Mail Pouch Tobacco barn ads on Indiana's State Route 62 in Lanesville, **top and right**, and Minerva, Ohio on the Lincoln Highway, **left**, are in different states of repair.

Clockwise from top: A Mail Pouch ad on the Lincoln Highway near Canton, Ohio; a Kentucky Club Pipe Tobacco ad in the same area; a Mail Pouch ad on U.S. Highway 52 east of Manchester.

Dr. Pierce's Medical Discovery is advertised in fading white letters on a barn off U.S. Highway 101 in California.

Mail Pouch was far from the only firm to make use of "the broad side of a barn" to hawk their wares.

Dr. Ray Vaughn Pierce used barns to advertise what he called his "Medical Discovery," a licorice elixir reputed to be tinged with opium, alcohol and quinine allegedly gave men a cowboy's appetite and an ostrich's digestion. Or his Vaginal Tablets. Or his Extract of Smart Weed. Or his Pleasant Pellets. Or his "Favorite Prescription" for "weak women."

Dr. Pierce's barn signs went up in the first half of the 20th century, until his company went out of business in 1940. (For more on Dr. Pierce and his signs, see my book *Highway 101*.) Like the Mail Pouch signs, they pointed the way to products available away from the highway itself. Other barn signs pointed to roadside attractions, giving drivers advance notice that something spectacular awaited straight ahead — or with a well-timed detour up a side road.

In 1935, Garnet Carter, the guy who invented miniature golf, started having barns painted with signs urging motorists to "See Rock City" atop Lookout Mountain in Tennessee. The site was known for two things: its immense boulders and the claim that someone standing there could see seven states from a particular vantage point. The truth of this is open to debate, but regardless, it was a great site with great views, conveniently located near where U.S. Highways 11, 41 and 27 came together in Chattanooga.

From the time it opened until 1969, Carter hired Clark Byers to paint more than 900 barn roofs and walls in 19 states. In return for the use of their barns, the owners received free passes to Rock City, along with swag. Or, if they preferred, they might get paid $3.

A Meramec Caverns barn is visible along Route 66 in Cayuga, Ill.

Another attraction that used barns to spread the word was Meramec Caverns, a natural underground network of tunnels and passages in the Ozark Mountains near Stanton, Mo. The caverns, reportedly once used as a hideout by Jesse James, opened as a tourist spot in 1935. After seeing a man's name on the roof of a barn, cavern owner Lester Dill decided to travel around and offer to paint barns for free — if their owners allowed him to paint the Meramec Caverns name on their roofs. At their peak, there were 400 billboards in 40 states, with 75 still in existence as of 2006.

Many other companies over the years have put up signs. The Highway Beautification Act of 1965, designed to crack down on eyesores along the highway, banned barn signs, but an exemption was passed nine years later that allowed "heritage" barns to continue.

And political signs, such as the one on North Carolina State Route 86, right, are still allowed.

Top: A dry goods company's sign on a broken-down barn along U.S. 52 east of Manchester, Ohio, is barely legible after having been largely washed away by the elements. **Above:** A sign on a barn in the Spencer, Mo., area along Route 66.

The kind of signs found on the roofs and slats of rural barns were often found in cities on the sides of brick buildings.

Top: Mail Pouch lettering is still visible on Tuscawaras Road in Canton, Ohio.

Left: A clothing sign on a Route 66 building in Grand View, Ind.

Top: A faded Coca-Cola billboard painted on the side of an old house on a stretch of Route 66 known as Garrison Avenue through Carthage, Mo. **Above:** Yukon's Best Flower in Yukon, Okla., uses the side of its own mill as a giant billboard along Route 66, with a lighted sign on top.

Actual billboards on freestanding signs, of course, were — and are — far more common beside America's highways than barns adorned with painted text. One of the most successful companies was Foster and Kleiser, formed in 1901 by George Kleiser and William Foster. In 1925, the company introduced a format that would become familiar to drivers up and down the West Coast: a billboard pane 12 feet tall by 25 feet wide, resting on a lattice base that looked like something you might see in a rose garden.

Streamlined Art Deco structures with rounded molding arrived a decade later, giving drivers a modern-looking symbol of hope amid the depths of the Great Depression. A series of lights situated over top edge of billboards illumined them for nighttime drivers.

Other styles also appeared, with innovations designed to catch the driver's eye. "Lizzie" billboards featured Greco-Roman statues of goddess-like women, standing on either side. In 1945, the *Los Angeles Times* won an award for a billboard that included a new daily headline to keep drivers updated on news from World War II.

As cars got faster, the messages got simpler and easier to digest at a quick glance. Quick-hitting slogans like Maxwell House's "Good to the last drop" and "You'll love a La Salle" became the rule of the day.

An old-style billboard, with lattice base, welcomes motorists to Carthage, Mo., on Route 66.

Top: Putting up a billboard in 1916 touting women's suffrage in Denver, Colo. **Above:** Billboards in Chicago in 1940, as photographed by John Vachon. *Library of Congress*

A pair of billboards from Foster and Kleiser line California roads. **Top:** A sign on a building along Highway 99, photographed by Dorothea Lange in 1937, hails the "world's shortest working hours," and declares, "There's no way like the American way." **Above:** A real estate ad touts farms for sale in Lee Russell's 1940 photo of an Art Deco billboard. *Library of Congress photos*

YESTERDAY'S HIGHWAYS

Top: Esso's famous slogan, "Put a tiger in your tank," appears on a billboard photographed in 1965 by Thomas J. O'Halloran.

Right: A Waco, Texas, filling station offers a variety of services on a sign captured by Lee Russell's camera in 1939. *Library of Congress photos*

Top: A stretch of road on Route 66 in Missouri shows a barn sign showcasing Meramec Caverns alongside a couple of more traditional roadside billboards. **Above:** Billboards line the highway beside U.S. 101 in Northern California.

YESTERDAY'S HIGHWAYS

Faded signs on Route 66 near Houck, Ariz., tout Native American jewelry, sand paintings, Kodak film and other products geared toward tourists.

In addition to big companies selling space on their signs, companies that owned large plots of land set up their own roadside signposts to let drivers know they were "just ahead" at the "next exit." The rapid, one-after-the-other sequence of billboards served two purposes: First, they allowed companies to advertise several different products; second, they made an impression. If you missed the first sign, chances were, you'd see the next one. And, if the sequence was long enough, you'd probably find yourself looking to see what the next one would say.

A succession of signs prepares drivers to exit at the Route 66 Casino and Hotel at Rio Puerco.

A Burma-Shave sign at the end of a sequence along Route 66 in Arizona.

The most famous of these sign series, however, didn't invite drivers to take the next exit. They reminded motorists (the men, anyway) to do something about that five o'clock shadow at the motel before they hit the road again in the morning — and to use one very specific product in doing so.

What was that product? Well, you had to wait until the end of the sign sequence to find out... unless, that is, you'd seen a similar sequence before. And if you were traveling across country in the middle of the 20th century, it was more than likely that you had.

Burma-Shave signs were just about everywhere back then. At their zenith, there were 7,000 of them in 45 states. The rise and fall of the company paralleled the birth and decline of the federal highway system: Founded in 1925, a year before the system was dedicated, the shaving cream company stayed in business until 1966, about the time President Eisenhower's interstate system had begun to replace it.

The signs weren't billboard size. The first of them were 36-inch pieces of wood set up along Minnesota Route 35 south of Minneapolis. And not all the signs bore the company name. Rather, they were arranged in sequences or five or six: The first several each contained the line of a short rhyme, with only the last revealing the sponsor:

YESTERDAY'S HIGHWAYS

"Burma-Shave." Many of the rhymes were pioneering public service messages, focused on safe-driving habits. Others related the perils of forgetting to shave: Bearded drivers, be warned. Read these from top to bottom:

SAFETY	**SHAVING**
Past schoolhouses	The bearded devil
Take it slow	Is forced to dwell
Let the little	In the only place
Shavers grow	Where they don't sell... Burma Shave
Train approaching	She eyed his beard
Whistle squealing	And said, "No dice.
Pause, avoid	The wedding's off
That rundown feeling	I'll cook the rice."
Her chariot raced	The poorest guy
At eighty per	In the human race
They hauled away	Can have a
What had ben hur	Million dollar face
Although insured	Said Juliet
Remember, kiddo	To Romeo
They don't pay you	If you don't shave
They pay your widow	Go homeo
Thirty days	To steal a kiss
Hath September	He had a knack
April, June	But lacked the cheek
And speed offender	To get one back

A Burma-Shave sign on 66 in Ash Fork, Ariz.

Company owner Clinton Odell and his sons, Allan and Leonard, had tried other ideas to market Burma-Shave, which wasn't the company's first product. The Odells had initially tried to sell a liniment they called Burma Vita: This was the era of "healing tonics and elixirs" — known to detractors as snake oil — and Burma Vita was based on an old family recipe. But competition was heavy, and if you weren't sick, you didn't need it. So, the Odells started looking for a product consumers would need every day, hoping to follow in the footsteps of colas that had transformed themselves from "elixirs" for the ailing into soft drinks for the masses.

They hit on the idea of shaving cream.

Burma-Shave, the original "brushless" (non-lathering) shave cream, was born.

But it wasn't an immediate hit. The family struggled to find a winning formula for marketing it, including a promotion they called "Jars on Approval." Odell's sons would visit men at their offices and give them a jar of the stuff. If they liked it, they could pay 50 cents the next time the boys stopped by. If they didn't, no harm done: The Odells would take back the unused portion, no questions asked.

Pounding the pavement like that took its toll on Allan, who thought there must be a better way to promote the family's new product. One day, he noticed a series of signs along the highway touting gas, oil and restrooms in order, then pointing the way to a roadside service station. He thought the idea would work for Burma-Shave, too, but his father was skeptical. Still, after some lobbying, Allan managed to persuade his dad to give him $200 for a pilot project to place a few signs 100 paces apart on a couple of highways in the Minneapolis area. They were an immediate success.

Encouraged, Clinton Odell spent $25,000 more to plant the signs all over the country, with the exception of Massachusetts (too many trees obscuring motorists' line of sight) and three southwestern states — Arizona, Nevada and New Mexico — that didn't have enough traffic to justify them.

A decade later, Burma-Shave was the No. 2 shaving cream in the United States.

The Odells wrote the first rhyming slogans. After that, they started asking their customers for ideas: Each year, they offered a $100 prize to anyone whose idea was accepted, and the contest proved so popular the Odells sometimes received more than 50,000 suggestions.

Sales flattened out after 1947, as cars with more powerful engines started traveling faster and zooming past the signs more quickly. The company increased the size of the signs and moved them farther apart, but to little avail.

Gillette bought the company in 1963. The roadside ad campaign was discontinued, and the signs themselves were taken down. The ones you see today are replicas, some of which, interestingly enough, can be found in Arizona — one of the states where they never appeared in the first place.

A sequence of signs along U.S. 101 near Gilroy, Calif., leads up to a roadside fruit stand.

From top: Billboards on Route 66 in Staunton, Ill.; in the desert Southwest; and in Shamrock, Texas.

YESTERDAY'S HIGHWAYS

Billboards were crucial to the war effort. During World War I, the image of Uncle Sam pointed his finger at passing motorists, uttering the message "I Want You for U.S. Army." (Little-known fact: The face on the image was modeled after that of the artist, James Montgomery Flagg.)

After the outbreak of World War II, many billboards directly touted the war effort — and encouraged those on the home front to do their part. Messages like "Buy U.S. Defense Bonds & Stamps Now" were everywhere, even as secondary slogans on boards that touted consumer products. An Auto-Lite Spark Plugs board, for example, proclaimed, "We're goin' to town fer Defense Bonds."

With content ranging from kitchen products to movie promos to political ads, billboards were everywhere. A 1914 display along West 63rd Street in Chicago consisted of a dozen or more billboards, placed end to end in a zigzag formation like playing cards. In 1926, a double-decker display of six Foster & Kleiser "lizzie" billboards stood next to six other standard boards along Market Street in San Francisco, touting products that ranged from Coca-Cola to the Pantages theater to Sunny Brook Whiskey.

By the 1960s, many billboards had adopted a cleaner look, with easy-to-read sans serif lettering, more contrast and more white space. The highways, however, were anything but clean. Critics had long declared billboards a highway menace: a blot on natural beauty and, they said, a threat to safety. Their sheer numbers were impressive — or distressing, depending on your point of view.

By 1950, there were more than 1,000 billboards on a 300-mile stretch of U.S. Route 1 in Florida. And that wasn't counting 6,000 signboards and 14,000 signs on trees and business places. The road between Baltimore and Washington was even more cluttered, with 2,450 commercial signs crowding a stretch of road just over 30 miles long. On U.S. 1 north of Philadelphia, a car traveling 50 mph passed a highway sign every second.

Congress got into the act in 1957, when a Senate subcommittee held hearings on the issue. Billboard groups were clearly on the defensive, telling lawmakers: "We do not create billboard canyons or ribbon slums on the highways." In fact, they said, billboards *improved* highway safety by providing visual stimuli to relieve the monotony of driving.

The critics were not persuaded. With a series of new highways about to be built under the Interstate Highway Act, they were convinced the situation would only get worse unless they acted.

They did persuade Congress to pass a bill that offered states an extra half-percent in highway funding if they controlled billboards. But it didn't work to stave off the proliferation of roadside ads.

Among those who took notice of the situation was Lady Bird Johnson, who sought reform "so you don't have a solid diet of billboards on all the roads." In 1965, her husband — President Lyndon Johnson — took up the cause, declaring in his State of the Union address that "a new and substantial effort must be made to landscape our highways and provide relaxation and recreation wherever the roads run."

The result was the Highway Beautification Act of 1965, also known as "Lady Bird's Bill." It limited the kind of signs that could be set up within 660 feet of a road to:

- Directional signs.
- "For sale" (or lease) signs on the property being offered.
- Ads for activities conducted on the property where the signs were put up.

Signs would continue to be allowed in commercial and industrial areas. The bill set aside $80 million over a two-year period to compensate billboard owners for the cost of sign removal. The federal government would pay 75% of those costs. An additional $240 million was allotted to states, so they could install landscaping and rights-of-way.

Local governments could use zoning laws to force the removal of signs without compensating their owners. But that changed in 1978 under an amendment backed by the billboard industry, which required such compensation. This happened just as federal funding for the program was beginning to dry up, which freed up companies to begin putting up more signs.

The law resulted in the removal of 587,000 signs from 1965 to 1985, but illegal signs remained, numbering in the tens of thousands. The General Accounting Office estimated it would cost $427 million to remove the 124,000 remaining illegal signs that predated the act... but federal funding for the program had shrunk to just $2 million.

Meanwhile, more signs were going up: By 1997, the number of new billboards was climbing by 5,000 to 15,000 a year. The upshot is that billboards remain a near-constant presence on the American road, informing and perhaps distracting motorists, blocking scenery... and making money for the companies that advertise there.

YESTERDAY'S HIGHWAYS

From top: Billboards in various states of disrepair on Route 66 east of Gallup, N.M.; on Route 66 east of Shamrock, Texas; and on U.S. 40 in central Missouri.

Faded trading post sign on Route 66 in Houck, Ariz.

Abandoned Places

A hollowed-out building in the Route 66 ghost town of Texola, on the Texas-Oklahoma line.

Falling Down

Highway bypasses leave some places behind, and sometimes, the owners of those places leave them behind, too.

Along Route 66, you'll find ghost towns like Glenrio on the Texas-New Mexico state line; Texola, straddling Texas and Oklahoma; Paris Springs in Missouri; or Amboy in the blistering California Mojave Desert. Elsewhere, towns survive but yield up the skeletal remains of old gas stations, motels, liquor stores and bowling alleys. Still other places have withered or died altogether, not because the highway has passed them by, but because factories have closed or moved on.

Some ghost towns are older than the highways themselves. The Pueblo of Laguna off Route 66 in New Mexico is a settlement of the Kawaik people that dates back to the 1400s. Many of the stone and adobe buildings still visible today went up at the tail end of the 17th century. The settlement was built around a lake with a lagoon (hence the name Laguna), which has since dried up. The buildings have nothing to do with the highway, but they're clearly visible from it, and you can walk up and explore some of them if you're so inclined.

Above: One stone building is visible from inside another at the Pueblo of Laguna along Route 66.

Left: Another stone building at the Pueblo.

YESTERDAY'S HIGHWAYS

Bodie, off California Highway 270 on the eastern slopes of the Sierra Nevada range, is a historic gold mining town that prospered in the last three decades of the 19th century. In 1879, it had a population of several thousand, but by 1915, everyone was gone. Today, it's a state historic park.

To the south, off Interstate 15 in San Bernardino County, lies a silver mining town called Calico that was home to some 3,500 people by 1890. But a new law driving down the price of silver spelled the end of the place by the turn of the century.

A different kind of boom led to dreams of a major development to the south, along what was then a section of U.S. 99 south of Indio (a stretch of road now signed as State Route 86). Developers saw the Salton Sea as the perfect place to build an American Riviera. If the desert landscape could support the likes of Las Vegas and Palm Springs, a new resort beside this massive "accidental salt lake" couldn't possibly fail.

Could it?

Well... The Salton Sea was formed in 1905, when the Colorado River overflowed its banks and rushed headlong into a natural depression. Over the years, the new "sea" attracted speedboat racers, vacationers and fishermen. But it also attracted pesticides, washed downhill from surrounding farmland and into the water, which grew more toxic and saltier as the years passed.

Developers who saw the banks of the Salton Sea as fertile ground for a new Shangri-La may have failed to notice this. Or they may have simply overestimated the demand for a place that L.A. residents could escape the smog and traffic. Either way, they built roads, streetlights and other infrastructure to welcome buyers they were sure would snap up lots along the "sea"-side.

Many lots, though, remained unsold. Others were purchased, only to be left vacant as the condition of the lake grew worse. Some people visited in campers and trailers, but left them behind to rot and rust, victims of the sun, the salty air and vandals who reveled in scrawling graffiti over every square inch of available space. Before long, the water was so toxic, dead fish started washing up on the lakeshore. Soon, the motels, shops and gas stations built to serve the resort-that-never-was closed up and fell victim to the elements — if they weren't torn down. (For much more, see my book *Highway 99*.)

Today, the Salton Sea is littered with modern ruins, fertile ground for photographers specializing in the surreal and a graveyard where big dreams once went to die.

Scenes from beside the Salton Sea.

YESTERDAY'S HIGHWAYS

In the California desert along old Route 66.

The shell of a 1902 stone building stands along Route 66 in the Plano Ghost Town, Mo. The first floor was a general store, with living quarters and a meeting room upstairs. There was a mortuary across the street, and a nearby stone building once housed a Tydol gas station. The small town was deserted when Interstate 44 bypassed Route 66 in the 1960s.

YESTERDAY'S HIGHWAYS

Top: Abandoned businesses along the Lincoln Highway in Roscoe, Neb. Chamberlin's was owned by Ben Chamberlin, who moved to town around 1910 and also ran a gas station and cabins on the site.

Above: This old train depot in Yukon, Okla., is now a storage shed.

A pair of abandoned homes offer distinctly different looks.

Top: The brick skeleton of a two-story brick home sits along Ohio Route 9.
Above: An old house is covered with vines along U.S. 29 in Chatham, Va.

YESTERDAY'S HIGHWAYS

From top: Remnants of old homes along U.S. 11 in New Market, Va.; Querino Canyon on Route 66 and on Indiana State Route 62.

From top: Old barns on Ohio State Route 11 and U.S. Highway 52 east of Manchester, Ohio.

YESTERDAY'S HIGHWAYS

From top: A small produce stand along U.S. 52 near Manchester, Ohio; a larger stand on Indiana State Route 62; and an abandoned block building (an old motel cabin?) along U.S. 58 west of Danville, Va.

The old Cascade Primitive Baptist Church sits abandoned in a small southern Virginia town.

Arrows

Hey! This Way!

Some of the entries in this chapter could have easily fit in other categories, but it was worth pointing out (literally) the role arrows have long played in roadside advertising. Plastic arrows. Neon arrows. Arrows with rows of cascading flashing lights.

Leading off this chapter is a photo of Henry's Drive-In on Route 66 in Cicero, Ill., south of Chicago. Bill Henry started the business in a trailer back in 1946 and built the permanent building four years later at 6031 W. Ogden Ave.

Arrows like the one on Henry's Drive-In are some of the most common symbols on the American highway, right up there with motel "(no) vacancy" signs and those lit-up martini glasses outside bars — and restaurants that have them. Arrows can be found on businesses of all kinds, from motels to movie theaters, from diners to drive-ins and more. Some are incorporated so seamlessly into the signs that surround them, you may barely notice them. Even though they're fast disappearing from the highways, the product of a largely bygone era, plenty remain along the roadside.

The selection on the pages that follow is just a small sample of what you'll find if you keep your eyes peeled and you know where to look.

The arrow at right is easy to spot on a flat stretch of road in Adrian, Texas, at the midway point between Chicago and Los Angeles — 1,139 miles each way — along Route 66. Built in 1928 as a one-room brick café, it was expanded in 1947 and was still operating as a café and gift shop as of 2019.

An arrow topped by a cowboy hat marks the Western Motel on Route 66 offers a glimpse of the past in Bethany, Okla., near Oklahoma City. There's not much history available on the place. The sign appears to date from the 1950s, and the motel reopened in 2014, featuring wi-fi and HBO in addition to the more standard "air conditioned" rooms.

YESTERDAY'S HIGHWAYS

Lim's Café in Redding, California, above, began on Yuba Street in 1933 and moved to Market Street — which was then part of U.S. Highway 99 — in 1957. The diner-style restaurant founded by Peter Lim remained in the family as of 2019, serving Mongolian beef stir-fry for breakfast homemade wontons. Its colorful sign features neon stars, a thermometer, and (of course) a swirling arrow. At right, an arrow points to a forgotten destination on Route 66 near Shamrock, Texas.

Right: The sign at the Route 66 Casino in Rio Puerco, N.M. features two arrows — one pointing toward the casino and the other embedded in the ground.

Below: The arrow at The Luna Café on old Route 66 near St. Louis has both a martini glass and an arrow on its crowded sign (which also features a tiny lobster). The café in Mitchell, Ill., was actually built in 1924, two years before Route 66 and the U.S. federal highway system opened. It was one of Al Capone's favorite hangouts along the "Mother Road." It once had a giant neon moon on the roof of the restaurant, but that's gone now.

The Copper Cart emporium, top, was built as a diner in 1952 in Seligman, Arizona. The Ranch House Café once served Mexican food in Tucumcari, N.M., but is long since abandoned. Both signs can be found along old Route 66.

Clockwise from top: An arrow for a long-abandoned used-car dealership along Golden State Boulevard (old U.S. 99) in Selma, California; a separate neon arrow indicates the entrance to the Sunset Motel on Route 66 in Villa Ridge, Missouri; a cactus-themed sign for the Desert Hills Motel on 66 in Tulsa, Oklahoma.

YESTERDAY'S HIGHWAYS

Clockwise from top left: Arrows point the way to Southern Chicken Restaurant on U.S. 11 in New Market, Va.; the permanently closed Lemieux Café and Lounge on Main Street (old U.S. Highway 6) in Green River, Utah; and Chef's Drive-In, an "old school burger and hot dog joint" on Business 29 in Altavista, Va.

Clockwise from left: The Supai Motel on Route 66 in Seligman, Ariz.; the Stein Motel sign preserved at Wilson's Café on U.S. 62 near Evansville; the Cotton Boll motel sign on Route 66 in Canute, Okla. (the motel itself is no longer in business).

YESTERDAY'S HIGHWAYS

Clockwise from top left: The Glancy Motor Hotel in Clinton, Okla., has a big arrowhead but is missing an "L"; the Cowboy Motel in Amarillo, Texas, uses an arrow to underline its name; the sign to Grant's Café in New Mexico has a stylish, curving arrow. All are on historic Route 66.

The Garden Inn Motel at Illinois Route 37 and U.S. 51 in Cairo, Ill.

Sources

"59 years of smiles. And counting," ihop.com.
"90 Brilliant Burma Shave Signs," thewhynot100.blogspot.com, June 7, 2015.
"1905 Glidden Tour," vmcca.org, 2017.
"1970s Burger Chef *Star Wars* Funmeal!" starwars.com, Man 2, 2016.
"A New Interpretation for 'Little Black Sambo,'" npr.org, Dec. 23, 2003.
"A&W Restaurant History!" aw-drivein.com.
"Abandoned Relics of the Past in Roscoe, Nebraska," placesthatwere.com.
"About Lomma Championship Miniature Golf Courses," lommagolf.com.
Acker, Lizzy. "Oregon to Become Home to World's Largest Corndog," Willamette Week, wweek.com, March 15, 2016.
"Ambler/Becker Texaco Station," illinoisroute66.org.
Americanroads.us.
"'America's Finest': Alamo Plaza Courts," misspreservation.com, Aug. 23, 2017.
"America's Highways, 1776-1976," U.S. Federal Highway Administration.
Ascierto, Jerry. "Where Did the First Road Signs Come From?" magazine.northeast.aaa.com, Dec. 18, 2019.
Barksdale, Nate. "Fries With That? A Brief History of Drive-Thru Dining," history.com, Aug. 22, 2018.
"Barn History," seerockcity.com.
Barnes, Kathryn. "The rise and demise of Carpinteria's Santa Claus Lane," kcrw.com.

YESTERDAY'S HIGHWAYS

Basten, Fred E. "Great American Billboards," Ten Speed Press, Berkeley, Calif., 2007.
Bathroom Readers' Institute. "Uncle John's Bathroom Reader, Vroom," Portable Press, 2012.
Belsky, Gary. "100 Years on a Dirty Dog: The History of Greyhound," mentalfloss.com, Dec. 19, 2013.
Beauchamp, Marc. "After serving generations of North State families, future of Lim's Café uncertain," redding.com.
"Bent Door Café & Midway Station," route66times.com.
"Billboard Battle, Dropped in Ware, To Flare Anew," Knoxville News-Sentinel, p. C-1, Jan. 1, 1950.
"Blue-plate special," worldwidewords.org.
"Blue Swallow Motel: History,' blueswallowmotel.com.
Bourne, Jennifer. "Mr. D'z Route 66 Diner in Kingman, Arizona," inspiredimperfection.com.
Brandt, Whitney. "American Movie Palaces: 50 Living Relics of U.S. Film History," pastemagazine.com, May 10, 2016.
Bridgehunter.com.
"CAT Scale celebrates 40 years of weighing," catscale.com.
"Census of Agriculture: 1940," p. 22, usda.mannlib.cornell.edu.
"Cicero: Site of Henry's Drive In," theroute66.com.
Cinematreasures.org.
Chaffins, Greg. "The History of the Mail Pouch Tobacco Barn," gotmountainlife.com, March 21, 2018.
"Classic American Diner," rockandrolldiner.com.
Clifford, James O. "Freeway squeezes Giant Orange dry," Long Beach Independent, p. A-28, Oct. 18, 1973.
"Coleman Theatre," nps.gov.
Collins, Timothy. "'Seedling Miles' Grow Lincoln Highway," dailyyonder.com, Sept. 8, 2014.
Crandall, Ziemnowicz, Parnell. "The Growth and Demise of the Howard Johnson's Restaurant Chain," researchgate.net, 2005.
Cutolo, Morgan. "Here's the Real Reason Why Diners Look Like Train Cars," Reader's Digest, rd.com.
Deadmotelsusa.tumblr.com.
"Dinosaur Fever – Sinclair's Icon," aoghs.org.
"Dinosaur Kingdom II," atlasobcura.com.
Doby, Hal. "A History of the American Movie Palace," dobywood.com, February 2013.
Dodds, Eric. "Mad Men: A Brief History of the Real-World Burger Chef," time.com, May 19, 2014.
"Drive-in Station with Canopy," uvm.edu.
Eschner, Kat. "The Brief 1930s Craze for 'Tom Thumb Golf,'" smithsonianmag.com, Feb. 9, 2017.
Espino, Jenny. "Lights out for Gene's Drive-In," Redding Record Searchlight, redding.com, July 27, 2017.
"Fighter Plane Crash Gas Station," weirdca.com.
Fitzgerald, Craig. "If you were a '60s or '70s kid, you'll remember these gas station giveaway toys," bestride.com.
Freeman, Paul. "Abandoned & Little-Known Airfields: Central New Mexico," airfields-freeman.com.
Garcia, Catherine. "Dinosaurs Keep Watch Over Cabazon," patch.com, March 13, 2011.
"Gardenway Motel," route66times.com.
Garner, Scott. "From Ballrooms to Discos, Tracking 150 Years of Roller Rinks," curbed.com, Oct. 23, 2014.
Gelders, Jesse F. "Why Midget Golf Swept Country," Popular Science Monthly, November 1930.
"Getting Our Kicks: On the Road in New Mexico (Clines Corners & Tucumcari," amoralegria.com.
"Gettysburg Area's Most Unique Attraction," mistereds.com.
"Gilmore the Flying Lion," Smithsonian, airandspace.si.edu.
Gilmorestation.com.
"Glenrio Ghost Town," atlasobscura.com.
"Good Humor Buys Dari-Delite Firm," Oakland Tribune, p. 49, Sept. 6, 1962.
"Greg Odell '64 on the history of Burma Shave signs," yale64.org.
"Group Denies Billboards Clutter Roads," Richmond (Ind.) Palladium-Item, p. 13, March 27, 1957.
Haines, Ron. "Old Gas Stations – the Recycled, the Vacant, the Falling Apart," ronhaines.wordpress.com.

Hinckley, Robinson. "The Big Book of Car Culture," MBI Publishing, St. Paul, Minn., 2005.
Hart, Alan S. "Carquinez to Sacramento," California Highways and Public Works, September-October 1961.
Hasan, Syeda Tahsin. "15 Differences Between Bridge and Culvert," civiltoday.com.
Henderson, Lori. "America's Roadside Lodging: The Rise and Fall of the Motel," eiu.edu, 2010.
Henderson, Roberta. "The Enduring Curse of Billboard Blight," Louisville Courier-Journal, p. D2, Nov. 2, 1997.
"Highway Beautification Act of 1965," library.cqpress.com.
"History of Clines Corners," clinescorners.com.
"History of OOH," oaaa.org.
"History of the AAA Glidden Tours," exchange.aaa.com.
"History of the US Highway System," gbcnet.com.
Hoffman, Ken. "Fast-food firsts: The Pig Stand has quite a few," Newport News Daily Press, p. J3, Aug. 16, 1998.
"Horne's: Look for the Yellow Roof!" highwayhost.com.
"Interstate System," fhwa.dot.gov.
Jacobs, Dean. "One block of Seedling Mile still exists," Fremont Tribune, fremonttribune.com, Sept. 23, 2016.
Jackle, Sculle. "Fast Food," Johns Hopkins University Press, Baltimore, 1999.
Jones, Dwayne. "What's New with the Pig Stands – Not the Pig Sandwich!" crm.cr.nps.gov/archive.
Jones, Lazelle. "The Lincoln Highway: A Century Later," trucktrend.com, Feb. 17, 2014.
Kaszynski, William. "The American Highway," McFarland & Co., Jefferson, N.C., 2000.
Kenworthy, Tom. "How the Highway Beautification Act went by the boards," washingtonpost.com, Feb. 24, 1987.
Kindred, Don. "Meet Me at Tommy's: New Owners Re-Claim '50s Diner," sanclementejournal.com, May 29, 2014.
"Knoxville's Grand Entertainment Palace," tennesseetheatre.com.
Kovalchik, Kara. "11 Gas Station Premiums of Yesteryear," mentalfloss.com, March 11, 2014.
"Lady Bird Johnson," pbs.org.
Lamers, Chantal. "Gravitational Tourist Draw," ocregister.com, July 22, 2007.
Livingston, Jill. "Keep Your Eyes Peeled for a Giant Orange," livinggoldpress.com, 2014.
Longfellow, Rickie. "Ohio's Vanishing Covered Bridges," fhwa.dot.gov.
"Looking for a motel in 1933," historichighways.wordpress.com, July 14, 2007.
"Luna Café: A notorious Route 66 eatery once frequented by Al Capone," atlasobscura.com.
McGee, Jim. "Nebraska's Lincoln Highway 'seedling miles,'" Dundee Times, trafficforum.wordpress.com, July 2019.
Mertz, Lee. "Origins of the Interstate System," fhwa.dot.gov.
Meyer, Ferdinand. "Looking at Dr. Pierce's Barn Advertising," peachridgeglass.com, Dec. 20, 2012.
"Missouri Theater," stjoemo.ifno.
Myers, Dan. "Why Are Sliders Called Sliders?" thedailymeal.com.
Myers, Don. "9 Things You Didn't Know About Denny's," thedailymeal.com, July 10, 2015.
"National Highway and Glidden Tours," mhchistoricalsociety.org.
"Number of drive-in cinema sites in the United States from 1995 to 2019," statistica.com.
Nussbaum, Nancy. "The Passing of a Legend: Harley Warrick, the Mail Pouch Sign Painter," thebarnjournal.org.
"Old Lincoln Highway in Omaha," atlasobscura.com.
"Our Company History," company.clearchanneloutdoor.com.
"Paul Bunyan and His Pal, Babe the Blue Ox," treesofmystery.net.
"Pittsburgh was the home of the country's first gas station," thealmanac.net, Nov. 29, 2013.
"Plano," theroute-66.com.
"Portable Scales Detect Overweight Trucks," Popular Science, November 1929.
Potter, Isaac B. "The Gospel of Good Roads," The Evening Post Printing House, New York, 1891.
"Portland Paramount Theatre/Arlene Schnitzer Concert Hall," oregonencyclopedia.org.
Provost, Stephen H. "A Whole Different League," Dragon Crown Books, 2019.

YESTERDAY'S HIGHWAYS

Provost, Stephen H. "Fresno Growing Up," Craven Street, 2015.
Provost, Stephen H. "Highway 99: The History of California's Main Street," Craven Street, Fresno, 2017.
Provost, Stephen H. "Martinsville Memories," Dragon Crown Books, 2019.
"Pueblo of Laguna," nps.gov.
"Queen Post Truss: All You Need to Know," gharpedia.com.
Ratay, Richard. "The Wild Weird World of American Roadside Attractions," Literary Hub, lithub.com, July 3, 2018.
"Reinforced-Concrete Highway Bridges in Minnesota, 1900-1945," dot.state.mn.us.
"Richard's Lunchbox," Weird California, weirdca.org.
RoadsideAmerica.com.
RoadsideArchitecture.com.
Rotermund, Maggie. "Meramec Caverns Barn Painter Has Been on Top of His Game for 50 Years," emissourian.com, 2006.
Russell, Tim. "Fill 'er Up!: The Great American Gas Station," Crestline, 2013.
"Sale of roller rink puts town in shock," Gadsden Times, p, C-2, Oct. 9, 1986.
"Santa Claus," Weird California, weirdca.com.
Sawyer, Don. "History of Diners and Drive-ins," dinerdon.com.
Segal, Troy. "Art Deco vs. Art Moderne," thesprucecrafts.com.
Sewell, Kristina. "Spotlight on: Bill's Take Out," santamariasun.com, Sept. 27, 2012.
Sherman, Don. "Indianapolis Motor Speedway: Birthplace of Speed," automobilemag.com, May 12, 2009.
Sinclairoil.com/history.
"Sno-White Drive-In – '60s Dining," snowhiteshakesandburgers.com.
"Starbucks (Gilmore Gas Station)," laconservancy.org.
"State Motor Vehicle Registrations, by Years, 1900-1905," fhwa.dot.gov.
"State Line Café & Texas Longhorn Motel," route66times.com.
Stewart, Ben. "From Model T to Model 3: How Driving Changed Over a Century," popularmechanics.com.
Swartz, William P. Jr. "Early Virginia Railroads," The Mountain Laurel, mtn.laurel.com, September 1985.
"The Evolution of the Gas Pump," saferack.com, June 28, 2017.
"The Great Bridge," p. 1, Topeka State Journal, Jan. 1, 1898.
"The History of Self-Fueling," NACS, convenience.org, Feb. 1, 2014.
"The Rise of the Food Truck," restaurantengine.com.
"The Root Beer Float Was Invented Today!" headsup.boyslife.org.
"The Valley Turnpike Company," nps.gov.
Theroute-66.com.
Thibodeau, Denice. "Danville's Tiny Town Golf back up and putting," godanriver.com, Jan. 24, 2018.
"Topeka Bridge Collapses; 1 Dead," Ottawa (Kansas) Herald, p. 1, July 3, 1965.
"U.S. 101 – Arroyo Hondo Bridge," geocities.ws.
Vaught, Steve. "Lighting Up the Coast," paradiseleased.wordpress.com, March 16, 2011.
Van Pelt, Lori. "Eisenhower's 1919 Road Trip and the Interstate Highway System," wyohistory.org, Jan. 4, 2018.
"Vickery Phillips 66 Station," nps.gov.
"Virginia Railroads and Railfanning in 'The Old Dominion State,'" american-rails.com.
Wang, Olivia. "Rolling the Years: Moonlight Rollerway's Enduring Appeal," kcet.org, June 16, 2013.
Warnick, Ron. "Gardenway Motel Closes," Route 66 News, route66news.com, Oct. 31, 2014.
Warnick, Ron. "One of the Whiting Brothers dies," Route 66 News, route66news.com, June 12, 2016.
Warnick, Ron. "The Story of the KuKu," route66news.com.
Warnick, Ron. "The true story about the ruins at Plano, Mo.," route66news.com, Dec. 5, 2013.
"Was the Lincoln Highway the First Transcontinental Highway?" fhwa.dot.gov.
Waterman, Martin. "Feeling nostalgic? Now you'll rave! Here's the story of Burma Shave," backwoodshome.com, 1996.

Waymarking.com.
Weingroff, Richard F. "Celebrating a Century of Cooperation," fhwa.dot.gov.
Weingroff, Richard F. "From Names to Numbers: The Origins of the U.S. Numbered Highway System," fhwa.dot.gov.
Weiser-Alexander, Kathy. "Cherokee Trail – An Alternate Road to the West," legendsofamerica.com.
Weiser-Alexander, Kathy. "Harvey Hotels & Restaurants on Route 66," legendsofamerica.com.
Weiser-Alexander, Kathy. "Paris Springs, Missouri – Revival on the Mother Road.," legendsofamerica.com.
Weiser-Alexander, Kathy. "Valentine Diners Along the Mother Road and Beyond," legendsofamerica.com.
Weiser-Alexander, Kathy. "Where are the Burma Shave Signs?" legendsofamerica.com.
Weiser-Alexander, Kathy. "Whiting Bros on the Mother Road," legendsofamerica.com.
"What's happening to bowling?" whitehutchinson.com.
Whitaker, Beverly. "Early American Roads and Trails," freepages.rootsweb.com.
"What ever happened to the Burger Chef chain?" metv.com, July 31, 2018.
"Whiting Brothers Gasoline Stations," rt66.x10host.com.
"Whiting Brothers Paper Collectibles," rt66x10host.com.
Williams, Ben R. "Bob White Covered Bridge washed away," Martinsville Bulletin, Sept. 29, 2015.
Witsil, Frank. "Is bowling in its final frames or will it roll on?" Detroit Free Press, usatoday.com, May 10, 2015.
Wood, Andrew. "The Rise and Fall of the Great American Motel," Smithsonian Magazine, smithsonianmag.com, June 30, 2017.
"Worcester Lunch Car Company – American Eagle Café No. 200," scalar.usc.edu.
"World's Largest Catsup Bottle Web Site and Fan Club," catsupbottle.com.
"World's Largest Light Bulb," atlasobscura.com.
Wyatt, Bill. "No more roller skating in Henry County," martinsvillbulletin.com, Dec. 30, 2019.
Ybarra, Evie. "California's Haunted Central Coast," 2018, The History Press.
"Yolo Causeway," localwiki.org/davis.

The Hill Top Motel on Route 66 in Arizona offered the "Best View in Kingman" … but it was closed for renovations in this 2019 photo.

Photo by Samaire Provost

About the author

Stephen H. Provost is an author and historian who has written several books about life in 20th century America. During more than three decades in journalism, he has worked as a managing editor, copy desk chief, columnist and reporter at five newspapers. Now a full-time author, he has written on such diverse topics as American highways, dragons, mutant superheroes, mythic archetypes, language, department stores and his hometown. He currently lives in Martinsville. And he loves cats. Read his blogs and keep up with his activities at stephenhprovost.com.

Did you enjoy this book?

Recommend it to a friend. And please consider rating it and/or leaving a brief review online at Amazon, Barnes & Noble and Goodreads.

Also by the author

Works of Fiction

The Talismans of Time (Academy of the Lost Labyrinth, Book 1)

Pathfinder of Destiny (Academy of the Lost Labyrinth, Book 2)

Astral Academy

Memortality (The Memortality Saga, Book 1)

Paralucidity (The Memortality Saga, Book 2)

The Only Dragon

Identity Break

Feathercap

Nightmare's Eve

Works of Nonfiction

Highway 99: The History of California's Main Street

Highway 101: The History of El Camino Real (Spring 2020)

The Great American Shopping Experience (Fall 2020)

Martinsville Memories

Fresno Growing Up

A Whole Different League

The Legend of Molly Bolin

Please Stop Saying That!

Undefeated

Media Meltdown

The Osiris Testament (The Phoenix Chronicles, Book 1)

The Way of the Phoenix (The Phoenix Chronicles, Book 2)

The Gospel of the Phoenix (The Phoenix Chronicles, Book 3)

Forged in Ancient Fires (The Phoenix Principle, Book 1)

Messiah in the Making (The Phoenix Principle, Book 2)

Praise for other works

"The complex idea of mixing morality and mortality is a fresh twist on the human condition. … **Memortality** is one of those books that will incite more questions than it answers. And for fandom, that's a good thing."

— Ricky L. Brown, Amazing Stories

"Punchy and fast paced, **Memortality** reads like a graphic novel. … (Provost's) style makes the trippy landscapes and mind-bending plot points more believable and adds a thrilling edge to this vivid crossover fantasy."

— Foreword Reviews

"The genres in this volume span horror, fantasy, and science-fiction, and each is handled deftly. … **Nightmare's Eve** should be on your reading list. The stories are at the intersection of nightmare and lucid dreaming, up ahead a signpost … next stop, your reading pile. Keep the nightlight on."

— R.B. Payne, Cemetery Dance

"**Memortality** by Stephen Provost is a highly original, thrilling novel unlike anything else out there."

— David McAfee, bestselling author of 33 A.D., 61 A.D., and 79 A.D.

"Profusely illustrated throughout, **Highway 99** is unreservedly recommended as an essential and core addition to every community and academic library's California History collections."

— California Bookwatch

"An essential primer for anyone seeking an entrée into the genre. Provost serves up a smorgasbord of highlights gleaned from his personal memories of and research into the various nooks and crannies of what 'used-to-be' in professional team sports."

— Tim Hanlon, Good Seats Still Available, on **A Whole Different League**

"As informed and informative as it is entertaining and absorbing, **Fresno Growing Up** is very highly recommended for personal, community, and academic library 20th Century American History collections."

— John Burroughs, Reviewer's Bookwatch

"Provost sticks mostly to the classics: vampires, ghosts, aliens, and even dragons. But trekking familiar terrain allows the author to subvert readers' expectations. ... Provost's poetry skillfully displays the same somber themes as the stories. ... Worthy tales that prove external forces are no more terrifying than what's inside people's heads."

— Kirkus Reviews on **Nightmare's Eve**

"... an engaging narrative that pulls the reader into the story and onto the road. ... I highly recommend **Highway 99: The History of California's Main Street**, whether you're a roadside archaeology nut or just someone who enjoys a ripping story peppered with vintage photographs."

— Barbara Gossett,
Society for Commercial Archaeology Journal

www.ingramcontent.com/pod-product-compliance
Lightning Source LLC
Chambersburg PA
CBHW081915170426
43200CB00014B/2738